Praise for *The Prompts You Need to Help You Write the Book You Want to Write*

'The prompts in this comprehensive and deeply considered collection are an invitation to explore every aspect of the fiction-writer's craft. Reassuring and inspiring in equal measure, Burton's and Poster's long experience as teachers of creative writing rings out from every page. Used alone, or in combination with its sister volume, the book is a route to learning and embedding a rich palette of new writing skills.'
Helena Attlee, *author of* The Land Where Lemons Grow *and* Lev's Violin; *tutor for the Arvon Foundation*

'This engaging and lively handbook goes beyond setting exercises for writers, both aspiring and practising – it explains the how, the what and the why. It's like being in the presence of two experienced and enthusiastic tutors who are right there with you, every step of the way.'
Amal Chatterjee, Lecturer in Creative Writing, University of Oxford

'A perfect combination of techniques, examples, commentary and prompts – this book is like having two accomplished creative writing professors at your side as you hone your craft.'
Seth Clabough, Associate Professor of Creative Writing, Randolph-Macon College, USA

'A deft resource including expansive coverage of core elements of craft, together with highly generative exercises suitable for emerging and established practitioners. This text also offers exemplary support for teachers of literary fiction.'
Julia Prendergast, President and Chair of the Australasian Association of Writing Programs

'In this carefully structured and generously detailed book, each chapter leads the apprentice writer through increasingly advanced exercises and techniques. Thought-provoking examples stimulate the imagination and also illustrate the essential craft skills all writers need to acquire. Highly recommended!'
Jane Rogers, Fellow of the Royal Society of Literature, Professor Emerita of Writing, Sheffield Hallam University

THE PROMPTS YOU NEED TO HELP YOU WRITE THE BOOK YOU WANT TO WRITE

How can you take your writing to the next level? In this follow-up to their acclaimed handbook *The Book You Need to Read to Write the Book You Want to Write*, Sarah Burton and Jem Poster offer exercises and practical advice designed to set aspiring authors of fiction on their way to creating compelling short stories and novels. Carefully explaining the purpose and value of each exercise and encouraging writers to reflect on what they have learned in tackling each task, this themed collection of writing prompts provides both encouragement and inspiration.

There are many books of prompts already available, but this one is different. Its structured, in-depth approach significantly increases the impact of the exercises, ensuring that storytellers use their time and talent to best effect – not only exploring their own creativity but also developing a wider and clearer understanding of the writer's craft.

Co-founders of Cambridge University's Master's programme in creative writing, Sarah Burton and Jem Poster draw on a wealth of teaching experience in a variety of contexts, from informal community education to PhD supervision. Sarah is a novelist (*The Strange Adventures of H*, 2020), biographer (*A Double Life: A Biography of Charles and Mary Lamb*, 2004, shortlisted for the Mind Book of the Year award) and social historian (*Impostors: Six Kinds of Liar*, 2000). Jem is Emeritus Professor of Creative Writing, Aberystwyth University; he is also a novelist (*Courting Shadows*, 2002; *Rifling Paradise*, 2006), poet (*Brought to Light*, 2001) and literary critic/editor (*Edward Thomas, Prose Writings Vol. III*, 2018).

Sarah and Jem are co-authors of a handbook for fiction writers, *The Book You Need to Read to Write the Book You Want to Write* (Cambridge University Press, 2022) and a historical detective novel, *Eliza Mace* (2024). Together they run Between the Lines, an online mentoring programme for writers.

THE PROMPTS YOU NEED TO HELP YOU WRITE THE BOOK YOU WANT TO WRITE

PRACTICAL EXERCISES FOR FICTION WRITERS

SARAH BURTON
AND JEM POSTER

CAMBRIDGE
UNIVERSITY PRESS

Shaftesbury Road, Cambridge CB2 8EA, United Kingdom

One Liberty Plaza, 20th Floor, New York, NY 10006, USA

477 Williamstown Road, Port Melbourne, VIC 3207, Australia

314–321, 3rd Floor, Plot 3, Splendor Forum, Jasola District Centre, New Delhi – 110025, India

103 Penang Road, #05–06/07, Visioncrest Commercial, Singapore 238467

Cambridge University Press is part of Cambridge University Press & Assessment, a department of the University of Cambridge.

We share the University's mission to contribute to society through the pursuit of education, learning and research at the highest international levels of excellence.

www.cambridge.org
Information on this title: www.cambridge.org/9781009391474

DOI: 10.1017/9781009391481

© Sarah Burton and Jem Poster 2025

This publication is in copyright. Subject to statutory exception and to the provisions of relevant collective licensing agreements, no reproduction of any part may take place without the written permission of Cambridge University Press & Assessment.

When citing this work, please include a reference to the
DOI 10.1017/9781009391481

First published 2025

A catalogue record for this publication is available from the British Library

A Cataloging-in-Publication data record for this book is available from the Library of Congress

ISBN 978-1-009-39147-4 Paperback

Cambridge University Press & Assessment has no responsibility for the persistence or accuracy of URLs for external or third-party internet websites referred to in this publication and does not guarantee that any content on such websites is, or will remain, accurate or appropriate.

For EU product safety concerns, contact us at Calle de José Abascal, 56, 1°, 28003 Madrid, Spain, or email eugpsr@cambridge.org

For Sharon Williams,
a true friend

CONTENTS

Preface		*page xiii*
Using this book		*xiv*
1	Memory and imagination	1
	Where fiction begins	1
	Recollecting the past	2
	Alternative viewpoints	4
	Inventing the past	6
	Too much information	9
	Wider explorations	10
2	Character	15
	Defining character	15
	Minor characters	21
	Character development; conflict, consistency and contradiction	24
	Character and author	26
3	Structuring plot	29
	Introduction	29
	Developing plot	33
	Further development	36
	Delayed disclosure: hiding and revealing plot	40
	Checklist	43
4	Dialogue	47
	The challenges of dialogue	47
	What dialogue can tell us	49
	Conveying contextual and plot-related information through dialogue	50
	Dialogue as a means of revealing character and relationship	54

	Punctuating and attributing dialogue	57
	Bringing it all together	62
5	**Point of view**	**64**
	Definitions	64
	First-person viewpoint	65
	Third-person viewpoints	67
	Unreliable narratives	73
6	**Narrative voice**	**76**
	Definitions	76
	Narrative voice in first-person narratives	76
	Narrative voice in third-person narratives	82
7	**Beginnings and endings**	**84**
	Beginnings	84
	Endings	89
8	**Pace and tension**	**95**
9	**Description**	**108**
	Setting the scene	108
	Emotion in description	111
	Describing a character's surroundings	113
	Unfamiliar surroundings	115
	Familiar surroundings	116
	Appropriate description	118
	Describing a person's appearance	120
	The telling detail	122
10	**Research**	**124**
	The nature and value of research	124
	Using your sources	125
	Beyond the facts	131
	The world around us	134
	Investing in research	136
11	**Editing**	**138**

12	Wordplay	167
	Introduction	167
	The pleasure of words	168
	Letting go	169
	Constrained writing	171
	A bit of the proverbial	174
	Fun with puns	176
	Imitation games	177
	In brief	181

PREFACE

Welcome to this book. Perhaps you've picked it out from among the many books of writing prompts available because you've noticed that, while its title suggests a relationship with those books, its scope is much wider and more ambitious.

Most books of prompts consist *solely* of prompts: you are given one writing task after another and you simply have to complete each one before moving on to the next. This book does far more than that: it's a detailed guide, explaining the purpose and value of the exercises we give you and helping you to reflect constructively, with an eye to your future development as a writer, on what you've achieved in tackling them.

This structured, in-depth approach significantly increases the value of the exercises, ensuring that you use your writing time to best effect – not only exercising your creativity, but developing a fuller understanding of the writer's difficult but rewarding craft.

USING THIS BOOK

In our handbook for fiction writers, *The Book You Need to Read to Write the Book You Want to Write* (Cambridge University Press, 2022), we discuss a range of ideas integral to an understanding of the writer's craft. Those ideas represent one of the two main pillars of our teaching, the other being the workshop sessions, in which writers are given prompts designed to encourage practical engagement with key aspects of the craft. It's this practice-based approach that is foregrounded in the present book.

The prompts you'll find here correspond largely to the topics and issues discussed in *The Book You Need* and you'll naturally find it helpful to work with both books. However, the books are designed in such a way that they can be used independently of one another: each of the prompts in the present book is fully explained and contextualised, giving readers a clear sense of the purpose and value of the work they are invited to undertake.

We've structured the book along lines that make it easily navigable, but it doesn't follow from this that we expect all our readers to navigate it in the same way. Only the most methodical will want to address each exercise in sequence; many will browse, homing in on whatever seems generally interesting or potentially useful at the time of reading; others again may be grappling with a particular problem in their writing and will turn directly to the section relevant to their immediate concerns.

In describing these exercises as prompts we're deliberately steering you away from the idea of a narrowly prescribed task. The prompts you'll find here offer suggestions for practical engagement with matters central to the writing of fiction; each has a particular focus and each gives you a framework to build on, but you'll find you have considerable leeway in terms of your approach, and plenty of scope for original thought. Where there is no explicit guidance on a particular matter – for example, on whether to write in the first person or the third – this isn't an accidental omission but a reflection of our view that each prompt should allow ample space for exploration.

As in most matters related to writing, however, there's a balance to be struck. While encouraging a certain freedom, this book is also, of course, intended to offer guidance and direction: in addressing its exercises you'll find it helpful to keep the prompts in view and to follow their suggestions reasonably closely. It's always possible that one of these prompts will prove to be the starting-point for a complete short story or novel, a development that would inevitably involve wider exploration, but for our immediate purposes there's a value in focus and discipline. Apprentice practitioners in any art or craft will often concentrate on specific aspects of their work as a means of honing essential skills and deepening their understanding, one step at a time, of the enterprise as a whole – a young musician practising scales and arpeggios, for example, or an apprentice furniture-maker focusing on getting a dovetail joint right. Eventually the musician may step onto the stage to play a concerto, the furniture-maker may produce a fine cabinet, and in either case it's likely that the work will be all the better for the focused practice that preceded it.

You might consider, too, the apparent paradox that to be provided with a framework for your writing can actually be liberating. Certainly many who attend our classes find themselves writing more freely when they are given something to build on, and many appreciate the focus given to their work by being set a specific task.

We don't, in general, specify limits for the exercises, but you'll probably find it helpful to give yourself an approximate timeframe and wordcount for each one. Take as a guiding principle the idea that each exercise is ideally carried out at a single sitting, and bear in mind the important truth that more isn't necessarily better. In approaching the exercises you'll find it far more helpful to write a thoughtful and sharply focused passage of 300 words than to write 1,000 words of slack prose that fails to address, or addresses only tangentially, the matter in hand.

So before starting to write, take a little time to consider the prompt and its implications. Not too long – ten minutes should be plenty in most cases – but long enough to give you a general sense of purpose and direction. And when you've finished writing set the work aside, for a few minutes at least, before you read it through. This will give you a little distance from it, allowing a more reflective approach.

Reflecting on the piece you've written is an important part of the process. Which passages or elements seem to work well? What aspects of the piece might be improved? Are you able to pinpoint, or at least get a broad sense of, the reasons for any particular success? What might you do differently if you were to start the exercise again?

You don't actually need to start again, and indeed we wouldn't encourage you to spend time trying to polish the pieces you produce. Better to annotate them with any observations that seem helpful, file them away for future reference, and then move on. This book is designed to help you cover a lot of ground in a series of short bursts; getting bogged down in endless rewrites of the same piece will diminish the energy of your engagement with it. Good writers recognise the need to strike a balance between the desire to perfect their work and the knowledge that perfectionism can hinder progress; it's worth taking trouble over these exercises, but not to the point at which you lose momentum.

If you find you have a tendency to search out the exercises that seem easiest or that play to your particular strengths, bear in mind that although these may represent a good starting point, helping you to build confidence at an early stage, it's the tasks that initially seem the most challenging that will ultimately prove the most valuable as a means of progressing your writing; they may also prove to be a source of particular satisfaction.

Using this book

A note on gender: characters mentioned in these prompts are variously male or female. Our concern is emphatically not to direct your choice, but to offer plural possibilities: you should feel free to alter the names and gender of the characters as you see fit.

These introductory notes are here to serve as a guide, but in the end it's for you to find out, through direct engagement with the exercises, the ways of using the book that work most effectively for you – the ways that best help you to discover and enhance your skills as a writer.

– I –
Memory and imagination

Where fiction begins

J. R. R. Tolkien once observed that a story 'grows like a seed in the dark out of the leaf-mould of the mind; out of all that has been seen or thought or read'. The analogy provides us with a useful starting point, suggesting the interdependency of memory and imagination while also alerting us to the difference between them. The leaf-mould – the stuff of experience, laid down in memory – is essential for the growth of the seed, but the developing plant will be something different from the material in which it is rooted. The analogy can't of course be taken as a direct reflection of the complex ways in which fiction writers progress from the recollection of personal experience to imaginative storytelling, but thinking about its broad implications – its suggestions of nourishment, assimilation, growth and transformation – will help you towards an understanding of the nature and purpose of the exercises in this section.

All fiction is rooted in memory. We may not always recognise our own experience in our fictions (it's worth reminding ourselves here that, while some memories may be actively drawn from readily accessible levels of the mind, others may rise unbidden from deeper and darker reservoirs), but as writers we are all indebted to our memories. The familiar injunction 'Write what you know' presupposes an act of recollection; and although we shall be going on to suggest that the end result of a writing task may reveal something you didn't know when you started, it will probably be obvious to you from your own practice that recollected experience is the basis of fiction-writing.

We said at the outset that you should feel free to address the exercises in this book in the order you find most helpful, but in the case of this particular section there are significant advantages in following the sequence in which the exercises are set out. The section will take you, by gradual steps, from exercises that are firmly tied to your own experience through to exercises that necessarily engage the creative imagination. The idea is to show, firstly, how memory and imagination are related, and, secondly, how we can use our own remembered experience as a springboard, propelling ourselves into a wider imaginative space than memory alone allows.

Recollecting the past

As you move through this section you're likely to become increasingly aware of the difficulty of mapping the dividing line between recollection and imaginative recreation, but for the moment let's keep things simple, focusing more or less exclusively on recollected detail.

1.
   a) Think about a place you remember from childhood – preferably not your home, which may provide you with too much detail, but a place you visited regularly or, alternatively, a place that you may only have visited once or twice but which made a deep impression on you. Possible locations might be your grandparents' home, or a local park, cinema, museum or café; or you might recall an inspiring landscape or your first sight of the sea. For this exercise, focus on the detail of the place itself rather than on the people in it, writing down your recollections in note form in whatever order they occur to you.

   b) Think about a person you knew in childhood – preferably not a family member but someone with whom you had a more limited, though not unimportant, connection: perhaps a class teacher, a schoolfriend or the owner of a local shop. For present purposes,

> focus on the person's appearance rather than on their character
> or any interaction they may have had with you or others; we'll
> come to those matters later, but for now the task is simply to
> provide a portrait in words of the individual in question.

When you've addressed one or both of these tasks, take a few minutes to reflect on the process and the result. You may have found that you remembered more about your subject than you had anticipated when you began writing. Whether or not that happened in this instance, it's worth bearing in mind that the concentrated focus encouraged by an exercise of this kind can often stimulate memory, bringing buried material to the surface.

While we naturally hope that these two exercises held some interest for you, we'd understand entirely if you found yourself pushing at the constraints we've deliberately imposed. The piece you've written may well contain valuable detail but, assuming you followed the instructions we gave you, it won't tell a story. In Section 9 (Description) we shall address more fully the problems likely to arise with description that doesn't contribute to the development of a narrative; for the moment you may wish simply to note that, in the absence of a story, a series of remembered facts can eventually become tedious for both writer and reader.

So let's move on to our next exercise – still working with memory, but now with a story to tell.

2.
> Cast your mind back to childhood again, this time coming up
> with a recollection of something that happened to you – a specific
> incident, involving at least one other person. It may be a dramatic
> event, but it doesn't have to be: revisit any incident that has sig-
> nificance for you. Then write it down as you remember it.

As you reflect on the exercise, you may want to consider the implications of that concluding phrase, 'as you remember it'. Our recollections are seldom, if ever, precise. Were there any details of the recollected experience that seemed unclear to you? Was the sequence of events gapped or uncertain? Would your account be readily understood by a reader with no prior knowledge of the event you describe?

It's probable that, to some extent at least, you filled in gaps and clarified detail, recognising, whether rationally or intuitively, that the uncertainties naturally present in our recollections may need to be firmed up or reconfigured in the interests of a coherent narrative. And in that case you'll understand that you're already treading the hazy boundary between recollected fact and acknowledged fiction.

Alternative viewpoints

With the benefit of an adult perspective you'll no doubt realise that others involved in the incident will remember it differently. You may recognise this scene: a family gathering; one person reminding the others of an experience from the family's shared history; another objecting that it wasn't like that at all, but like this.... Such conversations remind us not simply of the fallibility of memory but of the way our memories are coloured by the quirks and limitations of our own particular viewpoint.

The child's view is often sharper and more immediate than the adult's, but it's also limited by a lack of experience and understanding. The adult view of an incident is likely to be characterised by a broader sense of context (this provides the backstory of a developed narrative) and a greater awareness of the views and feelings of others (providing scope for the exploration of character). With this in mind, let's move on to the next exercise, which will take you a step further from your own experience and a step closer to the writing of imaginative fiction.

This next exercise asks you to revisit the incident you've just described, but changing the point of view to that of someone else who was present. You can't know for sure what their experience was so you'll be asked to imagine this. Here's a hypothetical example, not intended to divert you from your own recollection, but simply to offer a useful illustration. Let's say your piece of writing recounted an occasion when you were asked to look after your younger brother in the garden. While you were searching for his scooter in the garage he opened the gate and went into the street. By the time you found the scooter he was nowhere to be seen. You ran in to tell your mother what had happened. She was furious with you, and although, after a search, your brother turned up safe and well in a neighbour's garden, her anger continued, casting a shadow over the whole morning.

Your initial recollection of the incident might have focused on the perceived unfairness of your mother's treatment of you. In searching for your brother's scooter weren't you simply trying to find a way of keeping him happily occupied, as your mother had suggested? Was it your fault if your brother had ignored your injunction to stay where he was while you went to the garage? And he hadn't come to any harm, had he? Why couldn't your mother have dropped the matter once he was found?

Now consider the incident from the mother's point of view. Think of her panic as she imagines what might have happened to her son. Has he been abducted? Hit by a car? Has he wandered down to the canal? Try to enter her mind as she runs up and down the street calling his name. For her, the quarter-hour before the boy is found seems an eternity, and the hours that follow are shadowed by self-recrimination, which she tries to deflect by blaming you.

Although the incident itself remains the same, you'll see that the second story is bound to be subtly but importantly different from the first, altered by the shift in perspective. When you come to write a short story or a novel it's worth giving careful consideration to the question of narrative viewpoint, asking yourself whether the viewpoint you're instinctively drawn to is simply the one that most closely conforms to your own experience. If so, experiment with other points of view, as this exercise invites you to do.

With these ideas in mind, you should be ready to tackle the exercise.

3.
Returning to the incident recalled in exercise 2, write a new version of the narrative, this time from the point of view of one of the other people present (or, if only one other person was involved, from that person's viewpoint.) In setting down your own memory of the incident you'll almost certainly have described the experience in the first person; now make the other person the 'I' of your narrative, addressing the same incident from their point of view. The purpose of the exercise isn't to establish what the other person *actually thought or felt* (that information may not be available to you) but to explore imaginatively what that person's experience of the incident *might have been*, and how it might differ from your own experience, as originally described.

As soon as we begin to imagine a remembered event from a new perspective we're pushing beyond our own experience into an alternative world. We may still be drawing largely on memory, but now something else is happening. We're inventing, refashioning; we're entering, however tentatively, the realms of fiction.

Inventing the past

When you look back over your response to exercise 3, you may find that the liveliest elements are those you've had to imagine. There's usually an energising excitement in invention, the thrill of stepping out into a world which, though necessarily derived in part from our own experience, is in some important sense a new creation.

The next exercise encourages you to take your fiction-making a step further, giving you licence to alter and augment remembered details in the wider interests of your narrative. You'll still be keeping in view the incident you used as the basis for the two previous

1 Memory and imagination

exercises, but this exercise moves you a step further from your own experience, encouraging you to explore more fully the ways in which the experience might be transformed.

By way of illustration, let's return to the hypothetical example used above, holding on to the core of the incident – the moment of inattention, the child going missing, the mother's frantic search – while considering, in broad terms, how a writer might amplify and shape that material to create a vivid and compelling piece of fiction. The possibilities are endless, but the following suggestions will help you to sharpen your focus on your own recollected material.

It's possible that you included dialogue in your original recollection of the incident, but more likely that you didn't: if speech figures at all in the stories we tell about our own past, it's usually in the form of reported speech. In the case of our illustrative example, we might expect something like this:

> *Mum began to shout at me, asking why I'd allowed it to happen, why I'd let him out of my sight at all. I told her it wasn't my fault, that I'd only been gone for a minute, but she wouldn't listen.*

One of the reasons we tend to avoid dialogue when we recall past events is simply that we don't usually remember, word for word, what was said. But that needn't trouble us when we come to represent those events in our fictions. We shall be talking more generally in Section 4 about the value of dialogue, but for the moment let's just see how the passage above might be improved:

> *Mum flung the dishcloth at me. 'What were you thinking of?' she yelled. 'I told you not to take your eyes off him.'*
> *'I didn't. Well, only for a minute. I just went to – '*
> *'You left him?'*
> *'I thought – '*
> *But she was already rushing down the path towards the open gate. 'You go that way,' she shouted, gesturing towards the high street. 'Check the gardens as you go.' She hurried off in the direction of the canal.*

The most obvious lesson here is that direct speech can provide an energy missing from reported speech. The imagined dialogue creates a sense of immediacy, allowing the reader to participate more fully in the experience described. And it's not only the reader who benefits: when a writer puts words into the mouths of her characters – when she gives them their voices and listens to what she has made them say – she is also likely to imagine the scene more clearly and in greater detail. In this instance the detail of the flung dishcloth grew out of, or alongside, the mother's angry speech, while the mother's headlong rush down the path suggested itself as an appropriate physical expression of the anxiety and impatience implied by her interruptions.

But in sending these two characters off in opposite directions, haven't we put an end to the possibility of dialogue? Not at all: we can continue to develop our fictional world as the needs of our story dictate, perhaps sending the older child into the garden of an elderly widow who stubbornly refuses to allow a search of her premises; or into the garden of a young mother whose sympathy and well-meaning questions hold up the search while the minutes tick away. These characters may have no counterpart in the original incident, but their imagined voices can enrich this new narrative.

While these examples show how we can modify our material to create opportunities for dialogue, they also lead us on to another question you might want to consider as you reconfigure your own childhood memory: how can we catch and hold the attention of our readers? The 'lost child' incident is by its nature dramatic, but the way we shape the story in our telling of it will determine the level of tension and suspense, and therefore the degree to which readers are involved in the drama. If our protagonist walks into the street, hears the lost child calling from a garden, goes through the garden gate and finds him, we have a happy ending but a slender and unengaging story. If, on the other hand, we set up obstacles to the discovery, deferring and perhaps even throwing into doubt the happy outcome, we're likely to engage the reader more fully.

The point is obvious enough, and indeed you may realise that, even when casually recounting the events of the day to a group of friends or a family member, you're naturally inclined to shape and elaborate your material in the interests of holding your audience's attention. But it's also the case that our memories can keep us in thrall, tying us closely to the facts – or what we remember as the facts – when our narrative might be better served by a looser relationship with them. As writers of fiction we need to give ourselves licence to slacken the ties, to move beyond our own particular experience into a world of expanded possibility.

4.
Return to the incident recollected in exercises 2 and 3. Write a narrative that retains the core of the incident but departs from the surrounding detail in whatever ways best serve your story.

Too much information

When we revisit a childhood experience we often find that the passage of time has worn it down, in memory, to its essentials; if that's the case, our shaping of it will be primarily a matter of addition and elaboration. But not all memories have been refined in this way, and we may sometimes find ourselves dealing with a large amount of remembered material, not all of it helpful to our narrative. The memory of an incident that took place yesterday may be as valuable a resource as the memory of a childhood incident, but our approach to it will probably have to be more actively selective. The next exercise encourages you to think about the shedding of unhelpful detail in the interests of a well-shaped story.

For example, let's suppose you remember that one of two other people involved in the incident was sitting on a pale blue button-back sofa, leaning on an embroidered cushion, holding a pencil in one hand and a notebook in the other. Of course detail can add colour and life to a scene, but you might ask yourself whether your narrative is well served by the inclusion of all of these details; you may even come to see that the person on the sofa plays so small a part that he can be omitted from the narrative entirely, and that your story, far from being damaged by the omission, is enhanced by it.

5.
> **First, take a few minutes to set out in note form what you recall of a recent incident in which you were involved. Jot down the details as they come to you, without at this stage worrying about their order or their relative importance.**
>
> **When you've done this, write a narrative that takes the notes as its core material; as in exercise 4, you should feel free to invent detail. With an awareness of how details serve (or don't serve) the story, think carefully about what can be left out as well as what might be included.**

You may have become aware as you worked on this exercise that the sharp focus on what is to be omitted is a little artificial: we're highlighting for illustrative purposes a matter that can't, in practice, be neatly separated from other aspects of the shaping process. We can't say of any particular detail that it's *inherently* unusable: the decision to omit it – or to retain it – is dependent on its relationship with everything else that goes into the making of the narrative.

Wider explorations

Stored in our own minds are the memories transmitted to us by others – your mother's account of an incident from her schooldays, perhaps, or your grandfather's account of his wartime experience. Such memories can be a particularly valuable resource for the fiction writer. You'll have your own examples, and may want to explore these later, but for present purposes we'll focus on the memories provided below. These are designed to stimulate your imagination, not to provide you with a ready-made story.

1 Memory and imagination

a) *Three of us were walking along a path through woodland on the outskirts of a village not far from where we lived. We were schoolfriends, teenagers. It was evening and the light was beginning to fade. We looked up, just in time to see an old-fashioned cart crossing our path a little way ahead. When we reached the place at which it had crossed we saw that there was no path running at right angles to our own, just trees, growing too densely to allow a cart to pass through at any point.*

b) *When I was a child we lived in an isolated rural area. One afternoon, when I was about five years old, I was walking home from school with my mother. As we rounded a bend we saw that a motorcyclist had fallen from his bike and was lying, unconscious and bleeding, in the middle of the lane. Mum realised that the next vehicle to come along could hit him. She decided to stay in the lane to watch over him – it's hard to imagine now, but of course there were no mobile phones in those days – and sent me on alone to raise the alarm with a neighbour, half a mile away.*

Up to this point you've been working with your own memories, though at an increasing distance from the original experience; now, because these two memories are not your own, you'll need to make even more extensive use of your imagination. Although you may find this exercise more demanding than any you've addressed so far, you may also find yourself further liberated by the enforced detachment from your own personal history.

Detachment can't, of course, be complete: whatever you write will still be rooted in what you know. If, in our own lives, we'd never felt the shiver of the uncanny, if we'd never faced a dilemma like that faced by the mother, or been obliged, like her child, to undertake a difficult journey, we'd almost certainly find it difficult to deal with the material in these two exercises. But it's a safe bet that both of these recollections will correspond in certain respects to your own experience, and that the correspondences will help you to approach the material with insight and empathy.

These two memories may not be yours but the stories they inspire need to belong to you. Let's think further about the shaping process, bringing into focus the question of a story's meaning.

Set out as they are, more or less neutrally and with limited detail, the memories are largely undeveloped; in developing them it's likely – perhaps inevitable – that you'll be exploring the meaning they have for you, and shaping them in such a way as to bring out that meaning for the reader.

In the context of modern and contemporary fiction, meaning needs to be considered in subtle and complex terms: we're not speaking here about allegories or parables, in which one detail stands, more or less straightforwardly, for another, but about a broader and more elusive significance in the text – something that can't be accounted for by reference to plot alone. If someone asks what Joseph Conrad's *Heart of Darkness* (1899) is about, we might answer, in simple terms, that it's about a man who makes a journey up an African river to find a trader who has gone missing. That's not an inaccurate summary but it's a woefully inadequate one, mainly because it says nothing about the story's meaning. Early in the novella Conrad lets us know firstly that the tale *has* a meaning, and secondly that we shouldn't expect that meaning to be a simple one, easily encapsulated: its narrator, Marlow, is described as one to whom 'the meaning of an episode was not inside like a kernel but outside, enveloping the tale which brought it out only as a glow brings out a haze, in the likeness of one of these misty halos that sometimes are made visible by the spectral illumination of moonshine'.

You may not want your own meanings to be quite as nebulous as this, but as you address these two exercises, letting your imagination work on the bare outlines you've been given, you'll naturally want to consider matters of this kind, asking yourself a variety of questions. Will the story that arises from the first of these two recollections be an exploration of the effects of an encounter with the uncanny on three impressionable minds? Or, perhaps, of the effects of that encounter on two impressionable minds and one sceptical mind? If you choose the latter, you'll naturally introduce a debate: in that case will you inflect the dialogue in such a way as

1 Memory and imagination

to favour one or other interpretation of the event, or will you hold the two in balance?

As it stands, the recollection could be said to lack resolution, and the conclusion you provide may be crucial to your story's meaning: if your characters push through the undergrowth to discover a group of village children roaring with laughter at the hoax they've perpetrated using a prop from last year's school play, the meaning will be very different from the meaning of a story that ends with the three characters blundering back through the gathering darkness, terrified by their fleeting encounter with the inexplicable.

In the case of the second of the two recollections, attention to the child's thoughts and feelings – absent from the recollection as recorded here – might help you to think about your story's meaning. Does she set off in a state of high anxiety or does she see her journey as a thrilling adventure? Does something that happens during the course of the journey alter her feelings? Or perhaps her thoughts are focused less on the journey than on the injured man, whose plight gives her an early insight into the fragility of life. Alternatively, you might shift the viewpoint so that your story reflects the mother's thoughts and feelings as she stands in the lane considering the possibility that in seeking to protect a man she doesn't know she has exposed a member of her own family to danger.

6.

Taking what you need from either memory a) or b), transform the material in whatever ways seem conducive to the production of a well-shaped narrative.

When you've completed the exercise, look back over your responses to the whole run of exercises in this section. Can you see ways in which the increasing demands on your imaginative powers have progressively strengthened the work you've produced?

Before we move on to the next section, it's worth emphasising a point which, though particularly appropriate to our discussion of the imagination, has implications for your approach to this book as a whole. The writing of fiction requires us to balance knowledge, and the control that often comes with knowledge, against an openness to the largely unpredictable promptings of the imagination. These exercises, together with our explanations, offer a road map that will guide you on your journey, but they also leave plenty of space for imaginative exploration. Take the guidance in whatever ways seem helpful; use the space as fully as you can.

– 2 –

Character

Defining character

Advice to developing writers often encourages them to create a comprehensive dossier for each character; as a result, they may spend a long time establishing the detail of their characters' lives, cataloguing everything from their childhood pets to their favourite food. 'Before you put a character in a story,' advises Janet Burroway in *Writing Fiction*, 'know how well that character sleeps, what he eats for lunch, what she buys and how the bills get paid.' This kind of advice isn't entirely inappropriate but it can prove unhelpful when carried to extremes, firstly because writing the catalogue can become a time-consuming fetish or distraction; secondly because the advice encourages us to throw everything indiscriminately into the mix, regardless of its likely relevance; and thirdly because it tends to fix character at too early a stage in the process, when it should still be fluid, responsive to the wider needs of the narrative in which it appears.

We know that character and plot are interdependent, and if we try to create characters independently of story they will tend to appear flat and static. (This is a matter we shall return to later in this section.) We're also likely to be aware that some characteristics are inherently more important than others: the fact that your character is chronically insecure, or wildly overambitious, is almost certainly going to be of greater significance than the fact that he has a liking for strawberries or once kept a hamster. More subtly, we need to be aware of *relevance* to the story: do the characteristics in question have a specific point or purpose in the context of our narrative? It's legitimate to argue – as proponents of the detailed preliminary dossier tend to do – that we don't always know which details are going to prove important as our narrative evolves, but it's also fair to say that intuition or plain common sense might steer us away from arbitrary and potentially endless catalogues. The exercises that follow are designed to foster a more organic, more practical and ultimately more deeply exploratory approach to the creation of character.

Let's take as our starting point the idea of a character returning to the place in which she grew up. In the course of the story she will be forced to reappraise her understanding of the people and events of her earlier life there. At the end she will stay, or leave, or decide to see how things go. We don't need any more of a plot at this stage: we have the broad shape of a story.

As you consider the possibilities for this character, you'll be faced with immediate and specific questions relating to your plot. What's the reason for her return? A funeral? A wedding? School reunion? A charitable event? Curiosity? Settling a score? Laying a ghost? Details of this kind can be adapted to suit the developing story. You'll also be asking yourself more general questions. What is the emotional journey of your character? What is it in the past that has made her reluctant to return until now? What is her current perception of her life and how will that perception change in the course of the story? What are the story's fundamental themes? What do you want the reader to think or feel at the story's end? These larger questions are often the most important ones.

Spend a while thinking about this, until you have a sense of some possible answers to your questions. You don't need definitive answers in order to do these exercises, and you can – indeed, you should – change any details if you have better ideas as you go on. When you're ready you can move on to the first of your exercises in the exploration of character. Each of the three prompts in the following group gives you an opportunity to experiment with an opening in which your protagonist is the only character in view.

2 Character

1.
   a) Your story starts with your character travelling to the place in which she grew up. Write your opening scene, beginning ten minutes before she arrives and ending at the moment she gets out of the car or off the train or bus.

   b) Your story starts with her arrival at her childhood home. Write your opening scene, beginning at the moment her old home comes into view and ending at the moment the front door opens.

   c) Your story starts with her arrival at an event or ceremony in her hometown. She's late and has had to go straight there. Write your opening scene, beginning at the moment she arrives at the venue and ending at the moment someone speaks to her.

As you read through what you've written you'll hopefully find that your writing is strongly suggestive of your character's personality, whether this has emerged from her thoughts (both the content of the thoughts and her ways of thinking), the things she notices, her actions, or her appearance. The passage should give some sense of how this particular individual apprehends the situation she is in (or the situation she is about to be in) or, at the very least, how she views the world.

Did you experience any particular difficulties with the task you chose? You will almost certainly have been made aware of the restrictions imposed by any scenario in which only one character is present. This isn't to say that you should avoid single-character scenarios – sometimes we need them, and it's important to learn how to handle them – but the absence of other characters can make it difficult to maintain narrative energy. A great deal of what we think of as character is revealed – and often revealed as variable or context-dependent – through interaction with others.

The next group of prompts will give you the opportunity to explore the dynamic set up by your central character's interaction with another character. We'll have something to say a little later in this section about the extent to which minor characters might be developed in ways that allow them their own importance without distracting us from more significant characters and events; for the moment, just remain aware of your main character as the primary focus of the exercise. Make dialogue a prominent feature, but bear in mind that you're writing a passage of fiction, and that other elements are likely to come into play.

Imagine this scene: your character arrives at her childhood home and her mother comes to the door. What are her feelings at this moment? – these won't all be expressed as dialogue. Is she pleased to see her mother or does her heart sink as she remembers the circumstances of her departure from the family home? Does she notice changes in her mother? In terms of action and body-language, how does her mother greet her, and how does the central character respond? – a small gesture (or the lack of one) can reveal a great deal about a person's feelings. These are simply suggestions – you'll probably want to find your own narrative – but they indicate the kind of consideration that might give depth and colour to the scene you're about to set up.

2.
- a) **Your story starts with your character on the doorstep of her childhood home. The door is opened by her mother – or another family member if you prefer. Write a passage of dialogue and any narrative you need around it to make it work effectively as fiction.**
- b) **Your story starts with her arriving at the event she has returned for and meeting an old schoolfriend. Write a passage of dialogue and any narrative you need around it to make it work effectively as fiction.**
- c) **Your story starts with her on a train or plane. A fellow passenger strikes up a conversation with her about where she's going. Write a passage of dialogue and any narrative you need around it to make it work effectively as fiction.**

As you read through the completed exercise you should find that your rendering of this encounter has not only given the reader an impression of your main character but has also drawn energy from the presence of a secondary character; additionally, it may have set the ball rolling in terms of plot.

Another way you might inform the reader about your character is to start the story with her in her normal environment and have the prospect of the journey introduced. This enables you to give the reader some context, some sense of her life as it is before the journey that precipitates the main action of the narrative. The following group of exercises gives prominence to context as an aid to defining character.

3.
  a) **Start with your character in her normal domestic context and with someone else present – a friend perhaps, or flatmate, partner or child – when a phone call, email or letter brings the summons or invitation to the place where she grew up.**

  b) **Start with your character in her work context – perhaps engaged with a colleague or client in some particularly stressful activity – when the summons or invitation arrives.**

  c) **Start with your character in some informal social context – perhaps on a date, having drinks with colleagues, or engaged in some other group activity – when a text or phone call brings the summons or invitation.**

You have now imagined your character on her own, with people she has either never met before or hasn't seen for a long time, and with people she knows well in her daily life; you've been able to watch her at work and at home and in unfamiliar places. So you've seen her in the round, from different angles, acting and interacting in a variety of different contexts. You should have a much stronger sense now of who she might be, and this will help you fill out the bigger picture.

Hints have probably begun to emerge from these scenes about the cause or causes of her long absence and you may well have had some ideas about the reason for her return. In a sense the character may have started to direct the story – or at least to provide ideas for its future direction. Involving peripheral characters from her everyday life and from the place where she grew up may have given you more ideas to develop. In short, she has become, or is in process of becoming, a rounded character with relationships in and to the world. And, importantly, she now has a voice.

You may find it helpful to look back now over everything you've written about this character, noting what readers would know or might suppose about her from reading them. You might also note how your readers would have gained this information: have they been *told* or have they been *shown*? If, for example, you can see from your first piece that readers would know your character is indecisive, do they know this because your narrative has stated explicitly that she is indecisive; because she or another character has stated or suggested that she is indecisive; or because she has revealed her indecisiveness through the ways she speaks and acts?

If you've been learning your craft for any length of time you've probably come across the maxim *Show, don't tell*. That's too neat and sweeping a formulation to be entirely helpful – why rule out any means of communicating information to your reader? – but it's certainly the case that many developing writers do too much telling and too little showing, and that showing is usually the more effective strategy, particularly when it comes to representing character. In looking back over your responses to the prompts given so far in this section you may find passages that seem inert or unconvincing; if so, there's a strong likelihood that these will be passages in which too much is told and too little shown.

Fiction isn't life, of course, but it tends to work most engagingly when it feels like life. In life, we get to know what people are like by listening to what they say and watching how they behave; our understanding will also be influenced by what others say about them and how others behave towards them. When a writer lets a character emerge gradually in this way – through action and dialogue – the reader is more likely to be convinced by this than by a straightforward narrative description of the character. And this isn't only because the oblique approach reflects more accurately the way we learn about people in life; it's also because any writer who wishes to reveal character through speech and action will be obliged to *inhabit* that character, as distinct from merely observing her. The greater the writer's imaginative involvement with a character's life, the more authentically rounded that character is likely to appear to the reader.

Minor characters

We've already noted the importance of interaction between characters as a means of imparting energy to a narrative, and it may be helpful to think specifically now about the role of minor characters. They may not occupy much space within your text but for the duration of their stay they, too, will usually need to be presented as rounded, convincing figures. The discussion and exercise that follow are designed to encourage exploration of the life, views and feelings of a minor character.

Let's take as our two central characters a young man and his mother. The young man – let's call him Stefan – is a struggling artist who left home two years ago to get away from his overbearing parents. He has not met up with either parent since, but now his mother has come to see him. He has chosen to meet her in a café rather than invite her into his squalid flat.

These two characters will remain an active presence in the scene that follows, but we also want to introduce a minor character, the waitress who serves them. Would this work?

> *The waitress approached their table.*
> '*Good afternoon. What can I get you?*'
> *Stefan smiled up at her.* '*Tea for me, please. And a couple of slices of buttered toast.*'
> '*With jam?*'
> '*Just the toast.*'

> *'Of course.' She glanced at his mother. 'And for you, madam?'*
> *'A latte, please.'*
> *'Anything with it?'*
> *'No thanks.'*
> *The waitress jotted down their order and withdrew.*

The passage establishes the setting but it gives us nothing of the waitress's character. She's a cipher, a generic figure doing exactly what a waitress might be expected to do. If this is all we want from her, we might as well omit the predictable exchange by overleaping the scene: a phrase such as 'After the waitress had taken their order' would do the trick.

But we may be able to enhance our narrative by fleshing out our minor character. Although we don't need to know everything about her life in order to make her more substantial, we might find it helpful to imagine a few details. Suppose she's the mother of a child who has to be picked up from school shortly, and that she's therefore very conscious of the time; or that she has a splitting headache and has just been given a month's notice by her employer. Now we can begin to represent her as an individual.

> *They were barely through the door when the waitress came hurrying over. 'We'll be closing in half an hour,' she said.*
> *'That will be long enough,' said Stefan.*
> *His mother frowned. 'I don't think so, darling. We have a lot to discuss.'*
> *But the waitress was ushering them to a corner table. She tugged a cloth from her apron pocket and gave the surface a perfunctory wipe. Stefan pulled out a chair for his mother.*
> *'We can always go on to another café later,' he said. 'If we need to.' He sat down and took the menu from its stand.*
> *'I can save you a bit of time,' said the waitress. 'There's no cooked meals after two thirty. Tea, coffee, cake, scones – that's it. What can I get you, madam?'*
> *'I'll have a latte.'*

> Stefan glanced at the menu. 'Tea for me, please. And a slice of chocolate cake.'
>
> 'Chocolate cake?' said his mother. 'Chocolate always made you sick.'
>
> 'That's not true. You told me chocolate would make me sick, and for years I believed you.'
>
> The waitress was standing over them with her pencil poised. His mother scanned the menu. 'He'll have the Victoria sponge.'
>
> 'No,' said Stefan. 'The chocolate cake.'
>
> 'Maybe the lemon drizzle.'
>
> The waitress sighed. 'Surely he's old enough to make up his own mind.'
>
> Stefan saw the dangerous glint in his mother's eye and felt his stomach tighten. 'This is a family matter,' she said. 'It doesn't concern you.'
>
> 'It does if you make me stand here listening to you. I've got better things to do with my time.'
>
> 'You'd better mind your manners, young lady, or I'll be speaking to the manager.'
>
> The waitress shrugged. 'Go ahead,' she said. 'It's no skin off my nose.' She turned to Stefan. 'That'll be chocolate, then?'

The reasons for the waitress's behaviour don't need to be made explicit in the text – indeed, it's better that they're kept beneath the surface – but you'll see from this version of the scene how a few imagined details can help to give weight and texture to a minor character, while at the same time creating a stronger and more dynamic relationship with other characters. It's not that the minor character has become a major player – we understand that she may not appear again in the story – but that her brief turn in the spotlight has added significantly to the scene.

There is, of course, a danger that we might give too much weight to a minor character. If the waitress were to pull up a chair and, perhaps by way of excuse, tell Stefan and his mother about her unhappy childhood, her failed marriage and her fears for the future, this would give her plenty of substance but would almost certainly derail the main narrative. In this matter, as in so many others, balance is the key.

With all this in mind, let's turn to our next exercise.

4.

While Stefan and his mother are talking in the café the door opens and Stefan's landlady enters. Stefan has told his parents that he is making a success of his life, earning good money from the sale of his paintings; in fact he's in debt, with three months' rent owing. The landlady spots him and comes over to the table. What happens next? Spend a few moments thinking about her life and her preoccupations; then write the scene, building up a picture of this minor character and exploring the effect of her intervention on the two main characters.

When you've finished the exercise, look back over what you've written. Do you have a sense now of a character who, rather than simply disappearing once she has served her purpose, might be imagined as figuring in a different narrative? Have you, in other words, managed to breathe life into her?

Character development; conflict, consistency and contradiction

It will be obvious to any writer that, more or less by definition, plot can't be static; a little less obvious perhaps, but equally important, is the fact that our characters must be considered as similarly dynamic.

In the first place, plausibility demands that characters respond in some way to the events that form the plot. A character who discovers that he has been cheated by someone he had considered to be a friend is hardly likely to be unchanged by the discovery. Change might take place on two levels, the immediate and the long term: the character would almost certainly have to reconsider the friendship (even forgiveness would represent a shift, since he previously saw nothing to forgive) and, at a deeper level, his whole outlook on the world might be altered by the betrayal. To have him continue as though nothing had happened would be to keep plot and character inauthentically separate when they are, in practice, inextricably interconnected.

You'll be aware, too, that a reader's interest is much more likely to be aroused and held by a character who undergoes significant change than by one who plods along in a rut: there are, admittedly, works of fiction in which a particular character's unresponsiveness to circumstance is part of the point of the narrative; but, by and large, readers will want to see characters responding dynamically to their environment and to other characters. An interesting character will also often be one who gives evidence of the *inward* tensions and conflicts that beset so many people in life and which may well feature centrally in a work of fiction – think, for example, of Stephen Dedalus in James Joyce's *Portrait of the Artist as a Young Man* (1916) or Janie Crawford in Zora Neale Hurston's *Their Eyes Were Watching God* (1937).

You may have been told that a character must be consistent, and this is good advice – as long as we clearly understand the meaning and implications of the term in this context. We obviously want to avoid the kinds of inconsistency that make a reader lay down a book in frustration, saying of a particular character: *He'd never have done that.* But it follows from what we've just said that this doesn't – indeed, mustn't – exclude the possibility of representing a character who is in certain respects self-contradictory. We know that individuals in life will often reveal conflict and contradiction in their words and actions, and it's right that such things should be reflected in literature. What the frustrated reader probably means is that the writer has not provided the groundwork that gives plausibility to the contradiction.

Here's the bare outline of a story: a young woman cares lovingly for her invalid mother for a number of years, attentive to her increasing needs and putting her own life largely on hold. One day, in a fury, she picks up a kitchen knife and stabs her mother in the chest, killing her outright. We can't say that such a reversal couldn't happen – this is actually a bald account of an event in the life of the writer Mary Lamb – but the shift from carer to murderer will only be convincing to the reader if the complex circumstances that brought about the killing are revealed or suggested in the telling of the story. Few people, if any, behave arbitrarily in real life: it's when we don't know the relevant details of their stories that they may appear to do so. When one of our characters acts, as the phrase is, 'out of character', we need to make sure that the reasons for this are in some way incorporated in our narrative.

Here are two exercises designed to help you to think about these matters.

5.
   a) Prelude: it's parents' evening at a school. Melissa and her daughter, Louise, sit together, waiting to be called to see the teacher. Write the scene, giving prominence to their dialogue.

   They are called to their meeting with the teacher. At that meeting something unexpected is revealed by the teacher. You should decide what the revelation is, but there's no need to write the scene.

   Postlude: now write a second scene, in which Melissa and Louise are walking home after the meeting. Their dialogue may or may not address the revelation explicitly, but it will be coloured by it.

   b) Colin works in a busy office. He's a good employee, industrious and attentive to detail; he tends to keep himself to himself and, while not actually unpopular, is seldom invited to join in any discussions not directly related to his work. Write a piece in which Colin's character and habits are first established and then shown to be affected by a significant event in the office. It's up to you to decide on the nature of the event and, crucially in this context, the nature of your character's response.

Both of these exercises involve a plot detail – a trigger-event – but looking back over what you've written you should find that the event here is secondary in importance to your exploration of character and relationship.

Character and author

All fictional characters emanate from the mind of their author. This is true even when characters are based on people we know, or on historic figures whose lives we have researched: they are our imaginative framing of those real lives and therefore – whatever their origins – must be regarded as being, to a very significant extent, our own creations.

This said, we need to register the importance of establishing a distance between ourselves and the characters we create. While it's true that many fine works of fiction draw extensively on the lives of their authors, it's worth bearing in mind that one of the marks of the truly imaginative fiction writer is the ability to transform or transcend her own experience, creating characters whose lives, thoughts and personalities are very different from her own.

If every character in a work of fiction simply mirrors the personality and outlook of its author, the narrative will almost certainly lack vitality. We need, up to a point, to free ourselves from ourselves, to find ways of giving substance and plausibility to characters who don't closely resemble us. We need space to invent and imaginatively inhabit characters whose backgrounds differ from ours; whose gender or orientation are not our own; whose ideas and attitudes challenge or even contradict the views that we ourselves hold dear. Have you ever felt a resistance to letting one of your characters say or do something that goes against the grain of your own beliefs or personality? If so, you'll readily understand the purpose and value of the next exercise.

6.
> **Find a portrait that interests you but with which you don't identify closely (the website of London's National Portrait Gallery is an excellent resource, but of course you will find portraits on the websites of many other galleries) and write a brief first-person narrative in the imagined voice of the portrait's subject, keeping firmly in view the idea of depicting a character very different from yourself. Try to create a narrative rather than confining yourself to straightforward description (not, for example, 'I have a sad, pale face and am dressed entirely in black', but 'When they told me I was too young to commit myself to a life of mourning, I held**

my tongue'). **Don't concern yourself with the actual identity of the person in the portrait – this isn't a research project; simply use the image as a prompt to your imagination.**

We don't want to overstate the case. Your writing will always, to a considerable extent, reflect who you are: it's neither possible nor desirable to write from a place entirely detached from your own experience. However, as suggested in Section 1, it's worth exploring ways of easing the ties that, in binding us too firmly to the particularities of our own lives, prevent us from entering imaginatively into the lives of our characters.

– 3 –
Structuring plot

Introduction

When we speak of plot in the present context we mean the sequence of events of a story, presented in the order in which they are revealed to the reader. Since that definition may sound a little abstract, let's examine the plot of one particular story, 'Cinderella', which has the advantage of being very widely known. Its long history means that it exists in many variant forms, some more complex than others, but its relatively simple modern form can be easily summarised.

Cinderella lives with her stepmother and two stepsisters, all of whom conspire to make her life a misery. She slaves for them, receiving nothing but cruelty and contempt in return. One day news arrives of a ball to be held in honour of the prince. The two sisters attend, leaving Cinderella at home.

Help arrives in the form of Cinderella's fairy godmother. With a few flourishes of her magic wand she provides Cinderella with the accoutrements of a high-born lady of means, but warns her that the spell will wear off at midnight. Cinderella goes to the ball and dances with the prince, who is smitten by her beauty. On the stroke of midnight she leaves in haste, losing a slipper as she hurries away, returned to her former state.

She is tracked down, the dainty slipper proves to fit her slender foot and her story ends with marriage to the prince.

We can map the stages of the Cinderella plot on to a more broadly applicable scheme that highlights basic plot features common to many narratives, as follows:

The beginning of the beginning: establishing the status quo

'Once upon a time there was…' is the traditional opening that sets a story's protagonist in a particular place and situation. Here the world of the story is established and the protagonist introduced. This part of the pattern is sometimes termed *exposition*. (In the case of 'Cinderella' the place is the family home and the protagonist's situation is that she suffers abuse and oppression as the unpaid servant of her stepmother and stepsisters.)

The end of the beginning: disruption

Something happens that is going to change the situation. This development is sometimes termed *the inciting incident* or *the call to action*. (The forthcoming ball is announced.)

The middle: the main part of the story

The story is further developed through a sequence of events which are meaningfully connected and in which other characters usually play significant roles. This is sometimes termed *rising action* or *progressive complications*. (Cinderella's stepsisters go to the ball while Cinderella is left at home. She is visited by her fairy godmother who ensures that she is able to attend. She meets the prince and dances with him.)

The beginning of the end: climax

The main character faces a situation where events could go in their favour or against them. This is sometimes termed *crisis*. (Admired by the prince, Cinderella stands on the brink of happiness but her situation is threatened by the time-constraint of her fairy godmother's spell. The happy prospect gives way to humiliating flight and the apparent dashing of Cinderella's hopes.)

3 Structuring plot

The end of the end: resolution or open-ended conclusion

The consequences of the climax. The character has been transformed in some way and a new normal is established or prefigured. In a *closed ending*, the questions implicitly posed earlier in the narrative are answered; in the *open ending* more characteristic of modern fiction some matters may remain interestingly unresolved. This part of the story is sometimes termed *falling action*. (The Cinderella story provides us with a common form of the closed ending, with its protagonist's hopes being realised in marriage. The new normal for Cinderella is a radically transformed existence with the prospect of living 'happily ever after'.)

We shall return later in this section to the Cinderella story, but for our first exercise we're inviting you to test the broader applicability of the plot patterning we've just discussed.

1.
> **Think of a novel, short story or film with which you're familiar, preferably one you admire. Sketch out its plot in note form and then see if you can map that plot onto the basic plot outline above, in the way we've just done with the Cinderella story. Don't feel you have to force the plot to conform; the idea is simply to test *how far* it corresponds to the basic outline.**

Now look back over your response to the exercise. We can't, of course, know what text or film you chose, nor how closely it followed the contours of the basic outline, but the chances are that you recognised a significant level of correspondence between the two. Examining your chosen narrative, you were almost certainly able to identify both the setting up of an existing situation and, probably quite early on in the narrative, a change of circumstance that presents the protagonist with a challenge – an opportunity, for example, or a difficulty. This disruption and its effect on the protagonist (and probably on other characters too) is what propels a narrative into motion.

Your outline of what follows this disruption probably revealed a more or less universal characteristic: whatever the specific details, the protagonist's journey is hardly ever an easy one. Your chosen narrative probably presents as a sequence of events involving (in a broad sense) a series of advances and reversals. Circumstances and the actions of other characters will sometimes assist and sometimes hinder the protagonist's progress, and you may well have found this to be the case with your own example.

As you continued your analysis you were probably able to locate a point at which it seems that everything is on the line for the protagonist, who faces a major crisis. In fact, many stories have more than one crisis, but there is often a crucial test or turning point, more significant than the others, which tends to come late in the narrative and can therefore be properly termed a climax.

And it's quite likely, though by no means certain, that you found your outline concluding on a note of resolution. This matter is more complex because, as we've already noted, modern writers have tended to favour open-ended conclusions, and if your chosen narrative was – to take just two representative examples – Katherine Mansfield's short story 'Bliss' (1918) or Percival Everett's novel *Erasure* (2001), you might, not unreasonably, want to resist the idea that the conclusion of your chosen narrative resolves the matters it raises. While the protagonist of each of these works faces issues still unresolved at the story's conclusion, both narratives come to rest on an artistically satisfying note, and this might be viewed as a form of resolution; however, it's fair to say that resolution is not, in these cases, a feature of plot.

What is the value to writers, in practical terms, of identifying and mapping out these common characteristics? We should make it clear that our purpose in this section hasn't been to provide *prescriptions* for plot development, but to offer *descriptions* of recurrent narrative patterns, readily traceable in a wide range of stories. Once you've learned to recognise the patterns, you're in possession of useful knowledge: whether you choose, in your own writing, to conform to them, subvert them or actively defy them, that knowledge will help you to understand the nature of your task.

Developing plot

A large part of the writer's work is, in essence, the solving of plot-related problems and the recognition of plotting opportunities. The next exercise invites you to return to the Cinderella story, with a view to using its plot structure as the basis for a narrative of your own, though with a crucially different slant.

We suggested in Section 2 that characters help to create plot, but the story of Cinderella might be seen as an exception to this general rule. The reason is that Cinderella lacks agency; she doesn't propel the narrative forward because she doesn't initiate action. Events happen *to* her, not *because of* her. The family abuses her and she neither runs away nor fights back; faced with exclusion from the ball, she does nothing to remedy the situation – it's the intervention of the fairy godmother that makes her attendance possible; she doesn't pursue the Prince after the ball – it's he who seeks her out. Dutiful and beautiful but remarkably inert, Cinderella doesn't figure as a heroine in the way that, for example, Gretel does in 'Hansel and Gretel', cleverly outwitting the wicked witch to save herself and her brother.

In inviting you to accord greater agency to the Cinderella figure we're giving you a variety of problems to solve; you'll find it helpful to refer to the basic structure of the original tale, but you'll also need to address those problems for yourself.

2.
Ella is a modern woman, still living with her father, stepmother and two younger stepsisters though she is in her late twenties. Her home life is miserable and her menial job gives her no satisfaction.

Now, presenting these circumstances as the status quo and referring throughout to the structure of the Cinderella story

outlined above (but, importantly, not allowing yourself to be unhelpfully constrained by it), outline the story of Ella's struggle to assert herself and to find a more satisfying role in the world. What kind of life does she lead at home? What might happen at work – an argument? a new friendship? – that she can seize on as a means of changing her situation? What obstacles does she face? How does she overcome them? What critical event or circumstance gives her the reason or excuse for one final, decisive act? With what attitude does she confront the new prospect she has created for herself?

While most of the exercises in this book can be completed at a single sitting, this one may require more time.

In tackling this exercise you've probably been reminded that the individual elements of a plot can't be dealt with in isolation. You can home in on any one of those elements at any point in the writing process, but until the story is completed to your satisfaction everything is open to adjustment. Let's say, for example, that you decided early on that Ella works in the kitchen of a busy restaurant. But then you decide that the inciting incident involves a conversation with one of the restaurant's regulars, a young film director who, as it happens, is looking for a personal assistant. How is she going to meet him? You feel that the restaurant still works as a meeting place, but that you have to bring Ella out from the kitchen to work at the tables. So you go back and change her job: now she's a waitress.

That's how she meets the director – but why should he become interested, as the narrative develops, in giving her the opportunity of working with him? You come up with the answer: she shares with him an encyclopaedic knowledge of Hollywood musicals. The two characters naturally start talking and they bond over their shared passion.

Fine, but a convincing plot has to work for its revelations, large or small, and it will probably occur to you that you should have sown the seeds of this particular matter at an earlier stage.

Perhaps Ella's one solace in her otherwise miserable life has been an escape into the fantasy world represented by the films, and a proportion of her meagre earnings has been spent on DVDs bought in charity shops. So you return to an earlier point in your narrative and mention her interest there or, better still, create a scene in which that interest is revealed. Perhaps it occurs to you that her stepmother resents the time Ella spends watching the films, and this helps you establish the scene – an argument between the two characters.

This obstacle, placed early in your narrative, then gives you the idea for a later scene, one that sets up another obstacle to Ella's progress. You decide that Ella works under the watchful eye of a manager who sees her spending an inordinate amount of time at the film director's table; the manager threatens to sack her if she doesn't start pulling her weight. Now you move forward in the plot and add the scene; but having added it, you realise that you've placed it *after* the moment at which the director offers her the assistant's job.

What's the problem with that? Simply that it doesn't provide much of a crisis: from what we know of Ella we can assume that she will have no real difficulty in walking out of her current job into a potentially far more satisfying position. So you give her a dilemma and create tension by taking the scene back to an earlier point in the story, a point at which she is just getting to know the director. If she is sacked at that point she will probably lose contact with him; moreover she will lose the income that allows her to buy the films she loves. But if she restricts her interaction with him, in compliance with the manager's wishes, she also risks losing the connection. There's a third possibility: she can ask the director if she can meet him after work. But her natural shyness – which, you now realise, might require flagging up at an earlier point in the narrative – represents another obstacle. What will you have her do?

These plot details probably differ significantly from those of the story you've just written, but you'll understand the general principle we're illustrating here: the process by which a work of fiction is plotted must remain fluid, subject to repeated revisions in the interests of the narrative as a whole.

As we've already suggested, the basic plot pattern discussed above isn't a formula to be rigidly followed, but it may be a useful touchstone. If, looking back at the piece you've just written, you find passages that don't yet work as you'd like them to, you may find it helpful to test them against the pattern, asking yourself whether closer conformity to its contours might help to resolve the problems you've noted.

Further development

We're now going to move on to a new exercise, one that necessitates greater creative input on your part than the previous two, both of which drew on existing plots. All you're going to be given here is a bare stub; creating the rest of the plot will be an important test of your powers of invention.

Many plots have their origins in an actual event – something that happened to us, or perhaps to someone we know; or maybe the source is less personal – something we've come across in the media. As writers, we typically home in on an interesting detail and start to speculate about it. If our interest persists, we may then move into fiction-making mode and find that we are sowing the seeds of a viable story of our own. This exercise invites you to begin that process.

3.
> Select a news headline with the potential to spark a fictional plot – a starting point for your imaginative thinking. You may want to look for a headline yourself, or to work with one of the following examples, but whichever you do, we'd advise you not to engage too closely with the real-life story behind the headline: the idea is to take the prompt the headline gives you as the starting point for a plot of your own. For the purposes of this

exercise we recommend that you simply map out a broad plot outline; if you find yourself inspired by what you've begun here, there will be an opportunity to develop the material more fully in exercise 4.

Teacher's remains found buried under school after sixteen years (BBC News, 21 June 2019)

Author of How to Murder your Husband charged with murdering husband (Guardian, 16 September 2018)

They dated as teenagers. Forty years later, she decided to go on vacation with him (CNN, 14 April 2023)

Man gives children DNA test as joke but results 'ruin his life' (Daily Record, 28 June 2023)

Alabama hunt for missing prison inmate and guard (BBC News, 3 May 2022)

A woman gets twenty-one years for trying to kill her doppelganger with poisoned cheesecake (NPR, 21 April 2023)

As you consider what you've achieved in this exercise you'll perhaps recognise the satisfaction that comes as you begin to frame a narrative that is authentically your own, but you'll almost certainly feel that the task hasn't been an easy one: each step in the process is a step in the dark as you try to discern and chart the outline of a story whose successive stages don't exist until you have created them. For many writers, however, the most challenging part of developing a plot is what follows. As you'll already have understood from your engagement with exercise 2 and our subsequent discussion of that exercise, once you move beyond the basic outline of your plot and start to consider ways of delivering that plot you inevitably find yourself homing in on detail, investigating a range of choices as you amplify and consolidate the broad structural outlines of your narrative.

The ideas discussed in relation to exercise 2 are, of course, still relevant to our discussion, but we're now going to examine a further, related issue: the way outline plotting is developed into the more elaborate episodes or scenes necessary to bring our story to life. Screenwriters call these scenes *beats* and you may find the term useful as a way of distinguishing between the larger components of a plot outline and the more tightly focused elements by means of which the story advances towards its final form.

If we suggest that it can be useful to think in cinematic terms, we should probably add that it's almost impossible for the contemporary writer *not* to do so: modern fiction has been deeply influenced by the approaches and techniques used by film-makers. When you move on to the next exercise, you may automatically find yourself imagining the scenes as they might play out in a film.

Before addressing the exercise let's consider an example, based on the first of the news headlines above. The opening stages of an outline plot might run as follows:

> *In December 1962 a teacher in a small rural school walks out of his classroom on the last day of term and simply disappears. A reclusive man, he has been living alone in a rented room and has no friends in the locality, so it isn't until the beginning of the following term that anyone registers his disappearance. The police make perfunctory enquiries but find no trace of him, and it is assumed that he has simply left without giving notice.*
>
> *Sixteen years later a young man, Darren, reminiscing with friends, makes a connection that leads him to wonder whether there may be more to the story than meets the eye...*

If we want to create an effective opening scene, we must first identify our starting point. So far, so obvious – every story has to start somewhere – but deciding what that point is may involve considerable thought. In this instance you might consider beginning with the initiating incident – let's assume it's a murder – bearing in mind that, if you want your story to be a whodunnit, ending with the revelation of the murderer's identity, you'll need to withhold any information that might give the game away at the outset (we'll return to this matter later in the section). This option is likely to provide you with a dramatic opening; it's also true to the actual chronology of events – though, as we shall see, chronological sequence may be disrupted in the wider interests of a narrative.

You might decide to enter your story at a much later point, with the discovery of the body; again, this is an option with strong dramatic potential, but it sets up a practical problem – the need, subsequently, to deliver a heavy weight of back story. This problem isn't by any means insuperable, but we might find ourselves drawn to a third possibility, an opening whose focus is the conversation that reminds Darren of the teacher's disappearance and sets him thinking that some clue to the mystery may have been missed. Although this opening will almost inevitably be less dramatic than either of the other two, it has other advantages. If – as we might reasonably assume – Darren is to be the story's protagonist, this approach usefully establishes his centrality from the outset, while also providing an opportunity to set out, through the discourse of its characters, the essential facts of the case around which the narrative will revolve.

Let's see how this third option might be presented:

> Darren is chatting with friends in the pub when someone mentions the teacher's disappearance. As talk of the incident continues, he recalls his father, a building contractor, working in the school during the winter of 1962/3, laying a new floor. He remembers the year because of the unusually hard weather, and also because his father had brought home a lorry-load of quarry tiles from the school, arguing that there was no point leaving them there to be covered in concrete, and that in any case they had already been disturbed by someone else before he started the job. This last detail, forgotten for years, now begins to nag at Darren. He walks home brooding on the matter and eventually decides to question his father...

We're obviously still at the plotting stage here, with the opening a long way from its final form, but you can see how the plot is beginning to assume a more definite shape as detail is added. For the next exercise you're invited to work along similar lines, moving from broad plot outline to the mapping out of a specific scene.

4.

With the above example in mind, and taking as your basis the plot outline you created for exercise 3 (or working with another headline prompt if you prefer), sketch out a scene that might form the opening of a story.

When you've completed the exercise you should have a passage of writing that falls somewhere between your broad outline and a finished text. If you were to develop the scene still further (perhaps, to stay with our own example above, using the opening scene to give an impression of the atmosphere in the pub, or of Darren's character, or to set out the passages of dialogue that contain the expository information) you'd eventually find that plot was no longer your primary concern, though the broad plot outline and the scene-sketches would naturally have stood you in good stead as you expanded and elaborated your ideas. It needs to be emphasised, however, before we conclude this section, that most writers don't, in practice, approach their plotting in the orderly way we've taken as our model here; in fact, we'd go so far as to say that a rigid adherence to any particular method of plotting can be counterproductive. You may well find it helpful to have an idealised model for the development of plot, but you'll also need to register the importance of giving yourself latitude for creative manoeuvre.

Delayed disclosure: hiding and revealing plot

Anyone who reads detective fiction will understand the basic principle of delayed disclosure, and anyone who has tried to write it is likely to have a particularly keen sense of what is involved when – to take the obvious example of a conventional whodunnit – the identity of the criminal, as well as the means by which the crime was committed, must be withheld or shrouded in uncertainty until late in the narrative. In terms of actual chronology, the crime is the initiating event; in terms of the order of disclosure, the detailed explanation of the crime – the *dénouement* – is typically the concluding event. But the writer can't keep the lid on everything: he needs to provide the material that will advance the plot and also, in retrospect, be understood by the reader to have held important clues. Careful plotting can save you a good deal of time and trouble in the later stages of your story's development.

The detective story may provide us with the most obvious example, but the writing of a story in any genre will raise questions about the stages at which information is revealed: as we shall see in Section 8 (Pace and tension), part of the art of fiction writing consists in the ordering of plot detail to create interest and, in some cases, suspense.

Consider this plot outline – let's assume it's the outline for a short story, though it might equally well summarise a single incident in a longer narrative:

> *Daisy and Poppy are twin sisters. As children they were always dressed by their parents in matching outfits, but now they are in their early twenties and Poppy is irritated that Daisy still copies her style, often to the point of going out and buying exactly the same outfit that Poppy has just bought.*
>
> *Their parents' silver wedding anniversary is approaching, and a party is planned. Poppy deliberately misleads Daisy by hinting that she plans to wear her favourite floaty dress; in fact, she has bought a new red velvet jumpsuit for the event. But Daisy is coming to see that it's time she grew out of her copycat behaviour, so she buys an outfit different in every respect from Poppy's dress: a red velvet jumpsuit. When the big day arrives both sisters arrive at their parents' house in their matching jumpsuits.*

There's an obvious case here for a crucial piece of plot information to be held back until the end of the story. You can show one of the sisters buying a red velvet jumpsuit but if you show both of them doing so the effect of the final scene will be lost.

In addition to withholding information you may want to bury certain details, using distraction techniques to draw the reader's attention away from them. This will happen in any case as you move beyond the planning stage, adding detail to the bare outline of your plot: partially concealed among the preparations for the party – who is to be invited? is it worth hiring a marquee? will there be speeches? – the essential matter of the jumpsuit will come to seem less prominent than the initial outline might suggest. Even so, it's worth giving some attention at the planning stage to the ways in which important information can be simultaneously delivered and masked. If we return to the useful model of the classic whodunnit, the kinds of response we might ideally want to elicit from readers as they reach its conclusion are firstly, *I never even suspected her of being the murderer* and secondly, *Of course – the clues were there all along but I've only just caught on.* (When writing in this genre, of course, you might not only bury the important information, but actively include irrelevant information – red herrings – in order to allow genuine clues to recede further into the background.)

The following exercise invites you to work with these ideas to produce a plot that concludes with a revelation both prefigured in, and disguised by, the events that lead up to it.

5.
> **Sam considers his best friend, Steve, to be entirely trustworthy, to the extent that he's perfectly happy to let him go with his girlfriend, Lorna, to the pub or the cinema when his own work as a busy accountant prevents him from doing so himself. Your task is to plot a story that ends with the revelation that Steve and Lorna have been conducting an affair for months and have just got engaged. While you're unlikely to be able to ensure that this comes as a complete surprise to the reader, you can certainly mask the clues in such a way as to leave room for uncertainty up to the final reveal. You can do this in note form, but it might be helpful to provide some of the detail that will serve to prevent the reader from arriving at firm conclusions too early in the progress of the narrative.**

How did you approach this task? You may have decided to dramatise an occasion when Sam is unable to contact either Steve or Lorna while they are both supposedly in the pub; or you might have shown him walking into a room where the two of them are talking together, noticing the intensity of their conversation but (for reasons you might have mapped out in your plotting of the scene) misreading the signs; or you might have shown him catching some small gesture or look which momentarily puzzles him, or maybe registering, but misunderstanding, a hint dropped by a mutual friend. You might also have provided deceptive detail, perhaps by demonstrating Steve's apparent loyalty to Sam or his apparent lack of interest in Lorna. And as you developed your plot you may have seen it as an ideal candidate for an unreliable first-person narrative presented from Sam's viewpoint – a narrative in which the reader's inevitable suspicions are partially counteracted by the narrator's inability or refusal to see what is really going on.

Checklist

We'll conclude our discussion of plot with a checklist that you may find helpful as you continue to address this complex topic in your own writing.

Are all the necessary plot details there on the page?

This may seem a rather basic question, but it highlights a common problem. It's easy for an imaginative writer, immersed in the story he's telling, to visualise certain details so powerfully that they seem to be present in the written narrative when they are, in fact, present only in his mind. Check that your readers have all the information they need to follow the plot.

Does the plot offer a satisfactory account of your characters' motives?

Motivation can be understood in part as an aspect of character – is your character the kind of person who would do this thing? – but it's also an aspect of plot: does the plot provide a convincing reason for her to behave as she does? If you find a character doing something for no apparent reason (or for a reason that you, the writer, know, but which is not actually present in the outline) you probably need to go back to an earlier point in the narrative and sow the seeds that make the action, when it occurs, seem plausible.

Does the plot offer sufficient scope for character development and the exploration of complexities of character?

A static or unduly straightforward character doesn't usually make for an interesting narrative. Again, this is clearly a character-related issue but you can ensure, through manipulation of the plot details, that your character is challenged in ways that enforce self-appraisal, decision-making and development.

Have you created sufficient tension in your plot?

Is your protagonist's journey too straightforward? If most of the things she sets out to do are accomplished with ease, the story will certainly lack tension, and perhaps plausibility too. Most good plots set up obstacles to achievement; they also tend to give a sense of what the consequences of failure might be, and to make failure seem entirely possible.

Have you found the best starting point for your story?

Developing writers often begin their story at too early a point, focusing on detailed scene-setting and character description when they might more usefully immerse the reader directly in the action. Identifying the most appropriate point of entry isn't an exact science, but it's worth examining a range of possibilities to see what works best, and worth establishing that entry point at the plotting stage if you can.

Have you given sufficient thought to the order in which the elements of your plot are revealed?

Whether because our narrative constitutes a kind of puzzle (as in detective fiction) or simply because we want to pique our readers' curiosity and hold their attention, we need to think carefully about what is revealed, and when. Inevitably, questions of disclosure are also questions about what remains concealed, and for how long. It's worth noting that most readers expect to discover, in the course of a narrative, that what is initially withheld or masked will ultimately be revealed. Again, it's usually helpful to give the matter some attention at the plotting stage, even though you're unlikely to be able to work out every detail in advance.

Have you checked for loose ends in your plot, and tied up any that make the narrative appear untidy or lacking in consequentiality?

Not all narratives aim at neat resolutions, and some may derive much of their power from ambiguity and uncertainty, but a good work of fiction is likely to be plotted in such a way as to ensure that no significant narrative thread is simply left hanging as the plot develops. Relatedly, it's usually unwise to leave your readers wondering, at the end of a narrative, what has happened to anyone who has played a major role in it. This doesn't mean that you have to conclude by bringing your readers up to date on the lives of all major characters. Fictional characters may come and go in the course of a narrative, but it's a good idea to check that your plotting gives some sense of the reason for any character's final departure from the story.

The exercises in this section should have enhanced your understanding of the complexities of plotting, helping you not only to create and test a plot, but also to control the delivery of plot to the reader. These are matters of central importance: while a strong plot isn't in itself a guarantee of a good novel or short story, it can be regarded as the frame around which most successful works of fiction are constructed.

– 4 –
Dialogue

~

The challenges of dialogue

Many developing writers are anxious about dialogue. They worry that their representation of their characters' voices is unconvincing, and this can lead them to avoid dialogue wherever they can. It's quite possible that, in many cases, the anxiety is justified – writing sharp, convincing dialogue isn't always easy – but evasion is inadvisable, because strong dialogue is a crucial component of most good fiction. To hear characters speak is to be drawn into close relationship with them; conversely, long passages without dialogue risk alienating readers, holding them at a distance from the characters. This section is designed to help you to confront any anxieties you may have and to approach the challenges of dialogue with increased confidence.

A writer who is afraid of writing dialogue will often summarise a scene, reporting conversation rather than dramatising it, as in this passage:

> *Before he had even taken off his coat his mother told him his father had left. She said she didn't know where he was, or why he'd gone. David asked if she wanted a cup of tea, and when she said she did he went through to the kitchen and filled the kettle. He asked if anything had happened that day, whether they'd had an argument, but his mother didn't answer his questions. Instead she rattled on about how inconvenient it was, and how typical of him (though, as David pointed out, it wasn't typical at all; his father had never done anything of the kind before). It wasn't as if she was difficult to live with, she said – though the words were hardly out of her mouth before she was interfering in the usual ways, telling David he'd put out the wrong cups, complaining that he was using the expensive loose-leaf*

tea when tea-bags would be perfectly adequate. Eventually he lost his temper. He told her how impossible she was, and that he wasn't surprised his father had left. It didn't go down well.

The scene has considerable dramatic potential but the way it has been presented here severely limits its impact. It can be brought more vividly to life by the substitution of dialogue for reported speech. Refashioned as dialogue the passage might begin something like this:

> As he pushed the door shut his mother came rushing down the hallway. 'He's gone,' she said.
> 'Who's gone?'
> 'Dad. Just upped and left this morning.'
> 'Where is he?'
> She dabbed her eyes with a crumpled handkerchief. 'I don't know,' she said. 'No idea where, no idea why.'

Now over to you for the first exercise:

1. **Taking the sample opening provided above as your model, rewrite the whole scene, substituting dialogue for reported speech throughout to convey the information in more direct form. You don't have to restrict yourself entirely to dialogue – note the opening sentence and the crumpled handkerchief in the example above – but keep dialogue firmly in the foreground. Before you start, take a few moments to visualise your two characters and to 'hear' the individual quality of each of their voices.**

When you've finished the exercise, consider the result. Do you feel that your version is more lively and more engaging than the scene as originally presented? In shifting from reported to direct speech did you discover anything new about your characters – anything, that is, that you hadn't seen in them before you began the exercise? It's often the case that characters become more real to us, as writers, once we allow them their voices; and the more real they are to us, the greater the chance that they will seem real to our readers.

What dialogue can tell us

Having established that dialogue can add energy and immediacy to a narrative, let's consider, in broad terms, what else it can do. You may already have noticed that what characters tell each other will sometimes set up or advance plot, as in our version of the exercise above ('He's gone'), or here:

> *'You can't tell me what to do, Edie. You're not my mother.'*
> *'This isn't quite the way I'd intended to break the news to you, Henry, but as a matter of fact I am your mother.'*

Dialogue can also convey other kinds of information, as in the following two-hander, where the conversation provides context in the form of backstory – past events brought into the narrative present – together with insights into a third character, who is revealed (assuming the first speaker's claims can be taken at face value) as a hypocrite with a dubious past:

> *'Your dad and I go way back. We were at college together. In those days he was quite a lad, wild and a bit dangerous, usually in some kind of trouble.'*
> *'Really? It's hard to imagine. He's forever sounding off about the moral turpitude of Britain's youth.'*
> *'I know what I know. There was a lot of drink, a shedload of drugs, a few brushes with the law. And he used to keep a little book – all the women he'd had, with scores out of ten. It never affected his career, mind you, though it probably should have done.'*

You may already be aware that what is revealed in dialogue isn't necessarily restricted entirely to its content – to the facts it explicitly conveys; the manner in which characters express themselves may also be revealing. In the passage above, the main speaker is shown to be both garrulous and indiscreet, while the following exchange shows us one character who seems both aggressive and needy, in conversation with another who seems hesitant and evasive:

> 'You have to tell me, right now! Do you love me or not?'
> 'I'm not sure I... well, it depends what you mean by love.'
> 'Just answer the question – yes or no.'
> 'I think I do, but ...'

This is essentially showing, as distinct from telling, and in fact dialogue can often show a great deal in relatively few words. The following exchange succinctly suggests, without actually describing, both the type of location in which the exchange takes place and the unequal power dynamic between the two characters:

> 'Thanks for coming in, Clarkson. Sit down.'
> 'Thank you, sir.'
> 'I meant the other chair, but it doesn't matter – no, stay where you are. How are you getting on with the team?'
> 'Very well, thank you, sir.'
> 'Enjoying the work?'
> 'Oh yes, sir. Couldn't enjoy it more.'

And now, having established in broad terms what can be conveyed by dialogue, let's take a closer and more detailed look at the matter.

Conveying contextual and plot-related information through dialogue

In any work of fiction, some events are likely to take place – as it were – offstage. This is particularly true where a story is written in the first person or tight third person; in such cases the reader can only know what the main character knows and that character is unlikely to be present at every event that has a bearing on the narrative. This means that the reader, along with the protagonist, often relies on information provided by another character. For example, dialogue such as 'Jackie didn't come home last night' or 'Helen's been arrested' provides important information in succinct form.

However, succinctness isn't the only thing we're looking for. Consider a situation in which, in order to establish contextual details important to the narrative, you need to convey certain facts about an office worker and the company that employs him. Let's say you want to establish the name of the company, the department he works in, the name of his line manager and that the employee is new to the job. You might decide to handle this by having him called into the manager's office for a progress check and having the manager say something like this:

> 'Thanks for coming in, Mr Davies. How do you find working at Streamline Logistics? Are you settling in at Quality Control? How do you get on with Gina McColl, your line manager?'

This fragment of dialogue succinctly conveys the necessary information, but at the expense of plausibility. This doesn't feel like real speech: it's all too clearly an artificial device. Both characters know where they are working, what department the new employee is in and who the line manager is. This information would be unlikely to emerge in such crude form, so you'd need to find another way of conveying it to the reader. You can certainly do it through dialogue, but you have to be a bit more cunning.

When you're using dialogue to convey information to the reader it helps if there's something else going on in the scene, so that the information seems to emerge incidentally. This is, to put it bluntly, a distraction technique; however the distraction shouldn't simply be padding – which not only clogs the narrative but may also prove as unconvincing, in its own way, as the example above. Whatever we write needs a function, so it's important to consider what additional *necessary* function dialogue might serve here. Let's say that you want to convey that your character is keen to shine in this job but that his first attempts have the reverse effect. You can usefully combine that with the information you want to slip in, as in the following exchange:

> 'Thanks for coming in, Mr Davies. Sit down. How are you getting on?'
> 'Very well, thank you. In fact, I'm really glad to have this opportunity to speak to you. I've had some ideas for improving efficiency in the department.'
> 'Have you, indeed? I don't want to stifle initiative, but Quality Control seemed to be functioning perfectly well before you arrived. How long since you joined us?'
> 'Three weeks.'
> 'Not quite. According to my notes, just two-and-a-half weeks. A little early to be rocking the boat, wouldn't you say? Have you spoken to Gina McColl about your ideas?'
> 'Well, I thought I'd go straight to the top, and since I was going to see you anyway – '
> 'You have a line manager for a reason, Mr Davies. And there's a reason I chose Streamline Logistics as the company name. Efficiency through organisation. Demarcation, structure, process. It works.'

This passage does the two jobs we've given it, while remaining essentially plausible. It's always worth taking time to refine this kind of dialogic exposition, embedding specific detail in a more complex and more broadly informative interaction between the speakers.

You'll appreciate that we've also given the characters a reason for having this particular conversation. Dialogue can seem unnatural when no care has been taken by the writer to embed it in the story. A situation like the one we encountered in Section 2, in which a character meets an old schoolfriend after a long absence from her home town, can provide the opportunity for dialogic exposition of a kind that would sound unnatural if she had last met the friend two weeks ago; insistent questioning by one character might force another character to divulge a secret he would have been unlikely to reveal voluntarily.

Having a good reason for information to be conveyed is essential, and you should beware of crude attempts to justify dialogue that doesn't justify itself: it's not good enough to have characters half-acknowledge (with suspect lines such as 'Remind me why we're visiting your ex-fiancée' or 'Tell me again why you were cut out of your father's will') that they would probably already know what they're asking to be told. Writers have to work to find – or create – the opportunity for this information to be plausibly shared. Dialogue in fiction isn't exactly real speech; if it were, it would be full of repetitions, hesitations and unfinished or inconsequential sentences, none of which are likely to engage the reader. But it has to *feel like* real speech, and this means, among other things, that the speakers need to have good reasons for sharing the information the author wants their dialogue to convey.

You'll understand, from what we've said so far, that any reasonably extensive passage of dialogue is likely to work on a number of fronts simultaneously, and that this is not only unavoidable but desirable. The three exercises that follow are necessarily to some extent directive and focused on dialogue as a means of conveying contextual information; but our directions aren't intended to rule out a broader approach. See how much useful or necessary information you can convey in each case and how plausibly you can present it.

2.
  a) Write a passage of dialogue showing Marion and Jack processing the news that their son's flatmate, whom they have met on several occasions, is also his partner. In the process, you need to find subtle ways of incorporating the following information:

  – Marion is an only child
  – Jack is a retired police inspector
  – their son, Jamie, owns a badly behaved dog

  b) Marlene and Danny are discussing their very different ideas about how they should celebrate their mother's birthday. Their discussion needs to incorporate the following information:

- Marlene was adopted; Danny was born to their parents a year later
- Marlene has a more lavish lifestyle than Danny
- Danny is happily married, while Marlene is recently divorced

c) Terry is approached on the street by a beggar whom he recognises as Davy, a former classmate; Davy doesn't immediately recognise Terry. Write an exchange in which the following facts are revealed:

- Terry was bullied in school by Davy
- as a schoolboy, Terry was hopelessly in love with Davy's sister
- Davy once had a good job but lost it through no fault of his own

When you've finished take a little time to reflect on the dialogue you've produced. Have you managed to convey the required information in a way that sounds authentic? Does the exchange seem to you to maintain levels of interest and energy that would keep a reader fully involved while the information is delivered? Is there anything in your dialogue that reveals, incidentally rather than explicitly, the character of the speaker?

It's likely that you'll have answered the last question in the affirmative. Although your primary concern may have been the content of your characters' speech – the information you were asked to supply – the way your characters speak to one another will inevitably provide insights into who they are, both as individuals and in their relationship with one another. And that's the subject of the next group of exercises.

Dialogue as a means of revealing character and relationship

In Section 2 we touched tangentially on the part played by dialogue in defining character, and we're now going to sharpen our focus on the subject. The following passage of dialogue, though ostensibly about food, is more importantly about the speakers: it provides insights into the character of both, as well as significant information about the nature of their relationship:

> '*Are you going to sulk all evening?*'
> '*I'm not sulking. I'm tired.*'
> '*You're always tired.*'
> '*Can I get you something to eat?*'
> '*What is there?*'
> '*I made a meatloaf.*'
> '*I hate meatloaf. You know I hate meatloaf.*'
> '*Sorry. You said you liked it when your mum made it at the weekend.*'
> '*That was just for her sake. Isn't there anything else?*'
> '*I could make you bacon and eggs.*'
> '*Alright. But quickly. I'm hungry.*'

What can we deduce from this exchange? We might reasonably assume that the two speakers are a couple, or at least that this is a long-standing relationship. We might also see that beneath the explicit and rather superficial statements they make about themselves ('I'm tired.' 'I'm hungry.') there are deeper undercurrents, more obliquely revealed. The first speaker doesn't explicitly define himself as aggressive, petulant or self-centred, yet we're left in little doubt that he is all of these; the second speaker is, by similar means, revealed to be reactive, accommodating and averse to argument. The first speaker appears dominant in the relationship, though we might wonder whether the second character's relative steadiness is a sign of greater strength.

With this example in mind, let's turn to the next group of exercises. In each case, keep firmly in view the idea that it's better to reveal character *through* dialogue than simply to have the speakers provide the relevant information in the form of blunt statements. For example, 'I always worry about you, Suzi' will provide the requisite information in the first of the exercises below, but the statement doesn't offer the same interest, or potential for development, as 'Going out again, Suzi? What about your homework?'

3.
   a) Nora is trying to find out how her daughter, Suzi, is doing at school. Write a passage of dialogue showing that Nora is an inveterate worrier and that Suzi is rebellious and uncooperative.

   b) Fran is trying to get her older brother, Matt, to lend her £50. Write a passage of dialogue showing that Matt is by nature caring and helpful, but is concerned about his sister's spendthrift habits; show that Fran is obsessive about the image of herself that she projects to others.

   c) Leo has just come in from school and is telling his mother about an injustice visited on a fellow pupil by his class teacher. Write a passage of dialogue showing that Leo has strong views about justice in general, while his mother is inclined to focus on the practical details of day-to-day living.

It's probable – and understandable – that in responding, in limited space, to these rather specific prompts you've shown character and relationship as more or less fixed, but you'll be aware that in life character can often be (in a broad sense) unstable and relationship fluid, and that well-written dialogue may reflect this. Earlier in this section we looked at the example of an employee, Clarkson, in the manager's office and saw how dialogue might work to suggest a power relationship. That was a fairly simple example, moving along predictable lines, but dialogue may be more complex in its representation of character and the power dynamic between speakers. With this in mind, you might like to try the following exercise:

4.
   Harry Robertson is called to the manager's office to account for himself in the light of irregularities that have been traced back to the department in which he works. The manager strongly suspects Harry and intends to sack him but is hampered by lack of proof.

Write a passage of dialogue in which the power initially held by the manager is eroded, leaving Harry in control of the situation.

In addressing this exercise you'll have seen how dialogue can reveal the dynamic of a shifting relationship. The next two exercises are designed to help you explore the way in which characters may also, in dialogue, display the natural human tendency to adapt the things they say, and the way they say them, to different audiences.

5.
   a) **Write a passage in which Harry reports his interview with the manager to a group of friends in the pub. Feel free to have him change, omit or add details, and bear in mind that the passage is likely to be more interesting if you introduce interventions from his listeners.**

   b) **Harry's parents, who observe a strict moral code and would have preferred him to have followed his father into the teaching profession, ask him about his work in the office. Write a passage of dialogue in which Harry offers them a tailored account of the interview with his manager; again, interventions from his listeners may add interest to the scene.**

We discussed minor characters in Section 2. The dialogue you've just written should tell us quite a bit about Harry; does it also reveal aspects of the character of any of the friends or relatives to whom he describes his workplace meeting? If not, can you see ways in which your narrative might be enriched by giving fuller attention to the dialogue of one or more of these characters?

Punctuating and attributing dialogue

The purpose of all punctuation is to help make meaning clear, and an understanding of the conventions governing the punctuation of dialogue is essential for any writer of fiction. These conventions needn't be regarded as strict rules, but if you decide not to observe them, either in a particular piece of writing or more generally, you need to have a good reason for your decision, as well as considerable skill in avoiding the problems that non-observance can create. For present purposes we'll be working with conventional punctuation of dialogue: you may eventually want to experiment, but you'd be wise first to ensure that you have a sound understanding of standard practice.

The punctuation of dialogue is a code that enables the reader firstly to be sure who is speaking at any given point, and secondly to differentiate between the words spoken by the characters and the words that belong to the surrounding narrative. We absorb this code as we learn to read. However, many people who understand the code perfectly well when they read a work of fiction can stumble when they come to use it in their writing. If you're confident that you already understand the punctuation of dialogue, you should of course feel free to skip this subsection, though it's worth remembering that we don't always know everything we think we know.

It's likely that in addressing the exercises in this section you have already found it desirable or necessary to attribute dialogue – that is, to identify the speaker by the use of 'he said', 'she said' or '[character's name] said'. This probably applies particularly to exercises 5a) and 5b), both of which involve more than two characters. Where you have only two characters, attribution may be largely unnecessary; with three characters or more, it will sometimes be essential in order to avoid confusion.

The basics can be summarised fairly easily: a speaker's words are enclosed in inverted commas (normally single inverted commas in the UK, double inverted commas in the US) and the words of each new speaker occupy a new paragraph. You'll also notice from the following example that the full stop at the end of each speech falls within the closing inverted comma:

> *'I'm very fond of Avril.'*
> *'A little too fond, if you ask me.'*

The same principles apply when you supply an attribution, though the full stop is replaced by a comma.

> '*I'm very fond of Avril,*' he said.
> '*A little too fond, if you ask me,*' she said.

You'll notice that *he* and *she* don't take a capital letter here, for the logical reason that *Avril* and *me*, though still forming the end of the *speech*, no longer form the end of the *sentence*.

This basic pattern holds good when other forms of punctuation take the place of the full stop or comma, as here:

> '*Are you having an affair with Avril?*' she asked.
> '*Don't be ridiculous!*' he shouted.

When punctuating a longer speech, you may want to break it up like this:

> '*The trouble with you,*' said Jenny, '*is that you never see the obvious until it's too late.*'

Note the comma after *Jenny*, and note, too, that while it's usually neater, and more helpful to the reader, to introduce the attribution early on in a long sentence of dialogue (compare the nicely balanced sentence above with '*The trouble with you is that you never see the obvious until it's too late,*' said Jenny) you need to find a natural break in the sentence to accommodate it. You'll see immediately what's wrong with the following version: '*The trouble,*' said Jenny, '*with you is that you never see the obvious until it's too late.*'

Before you embark on the two final exercises in this section, it may be helpful to consider a few further points relating to attribution. Firstly, the use of 'said', as distinct from verbs which suggest the manner or function of the saying – for example, 'exclaimed', 'mumbled', 'expostulated', 'retorted'. Many people have been taught in school (perhaps with the laudable intention of extending their vocabulary) that plain 'said' is insufficient, but the general tendency in contemporary writing is to use 'said' as the default. The argument for 'said' is that it doesn't draw attention to itself, as the alternatives tend to do. Its function in dialogue is much the same as that of the inverted commas – a helpful signal to the reader rather than a means of elaborating the narrative. This doesn't mean that writers should never use any alternative to 'said', but our general advice would be to keep alternatives to an unobtrusive minimum.

Similarly with adverbs qualifying utterance – for example, 'he said *shyly*', 'she replied *angrily*'. These are often unnecessary – shyness or anger should ideally be recognisable in the dialogue itself. If you use them you should test them for added value and, again, be aware of their potential to distract the reader if overused. It might be added that some contemporary writers prefer to avoid them altogether.

Direct attribution isn't the only way of attaching dialogue to a particular speaker; actions can also help to locate it. Consider the following passage:

> *'Come and sit down.' We led Mum to a table by the window.*
> *'No need to hold on to me.' She shook me off and sat down. 'I'm not an invalid.'*
> *Hannah passed her the menu.*
> *She scanned it briefly. 'Nothing here I can eat. It's my teeth.'*
> *'How about some ice cream?' Hannah flashed her a dazzling smile.*
> *'That's soft.'*
> *'Too cold.'*
> *I sighed. 'Just tea, then. Earl Grey?'*

As you can see from this example, showing what's happening around the dialogue provides an alternative means of tying dialogue to its speaker, allowing you to vary the mix. And you'll perhaps have realised that there's another positive effect: using these actions in place of direct attribution encourages the writer to think more clearly about what else is going on in the scene and, by extension, to produce a more vividly realised narrative.

With all these points in mind, try the next exercise.

6.

The following scene is set out as a playscript, and your task is to turn it into an interesting and varied piece of prose. Your problem is that, while the playscript simply labels the words of each speaker, prose fiction normally makes the necessary attributions in more complex ways. With four speakers involved, this isn't an easy exercise, but taking up the challenge will give you useful practice in the punctuation and attribution of dialogue.

The dialogue is simply your framework: you will obviously have to add material in order to transform it in the ways suggested above, and you should feel free to extend your additions in any ways that contribute to the overall effect of your piece.

The scene: Sunday lunch at LAURA'S house. LAURA and her parents, MAUREEN and REG, are at the table. GEOFF, her new partner, places the gravy boat on the table and sits down.
GEOFF: *There. I think that's everything. Shall we say grace?*
REG *(reaching for the potatoes)*: *Grace.*
He shovels the potatoes on to his plate.
LAURA: *Dad! That's not funny – it's insulting.*
MAUREEN: *Reg, you owe Geoff an apology.*
GEOFF: *It's OK.*
MAUREEN: *It was rude. Go on, Reg. Apologise.*
GEOFF: *It's fine, honestly. Let's skip grace.*
MAUREEN *(awkwardly)*: *Lovely gravy, Geoff. Where did you learn to cook?*
REG: *Are you religious then, Geoff? Do you believe in all that stuff?*
LAURA: *Ignore him, darling.*
MAUREEN: *Did you go to catering college?*
REG: *Miracles? Angels? The immaculate conception?*
MAUREEN: *Don't speak with your mouth full. Honestly, I can't take you anywhere.*
GEOFF: *I just think it's good to be thankful sometimes.*
REG: *What for?*
GEOFF: *Everything. Food. A roof over our heads. Friends. Family. What are you grateful for, Reg?*

REG *(after a long silence)*: *I'm grateful that Laura found you. I'm glad she's happy.*
GEOFF: *There you are, then. More gravy, anyone?*

When you've finished the exercise, read it through. Does any part of your piece need to be altered or amplified in order to make clearer who is speaking? Conversely, can any of your attributions be omitted, or provided in more economical form, without causing confusion?

Bringing it all together

This group of exercises will give you greater freedom to develop ideas of your own, while putting into practice all you have learned about dialogue from this section.

7.
Below are four sets of plot points, all relating to the same event, a wedding reception. You can address any or all of the four tasks individually, as separate scenes; or you may want to create a more substantial narrative – a complete short story based on the prompts. You should feel free to take the narrative(s) in whatever directions you like, adding, omitting or altering detail; however, you'll be aware that the prompts are framed in such a way as to invite a strong focus on dialogue, and the voices of the characters should figure prominently in whatever narrative you produce.

a) The reception is being held at a smart hotel, and it's time for the best man (or any equivalent you choose) to give a speech. Perhaps he has already had a few drinks to steady his nerves. He lets out a piece of information about the groom during the speech (you decide what it is) that will be a shock to a number of people present – including the bride. Write a passage in which the speech is intercut with, and eventually interrupted by, the comments of two or three of the guests sitting in a group at a side table.

b) The groom has gone to look for the bride, who has left the room in tears after the speech. This leaves all four parents at the top table. An argument breaks out among them. It may be that each set of parents takes the side of their own child, but that needn't be the case. Your dialogue should reveal differences of character and/or attitude: perhaps one character has anger management issues while another is by nature a peacemaker; a third might resent the new partner while the fourth is inclined to see the good in everyone. You decide.

c) The bride is in a cubicle in the women's toilet. Unaware that she is there, two of the guests come in, discussing the revelation made in the best man's speech. After listening for a few moments the bride bursts out of the cubicle and confronts them, before rushing out.

d) The bride finds the groom alone in the garden. She asks him searching questions about the revelation and the groom answers her. Does he answer freely or under compulsion? Do the couple resolve the issue, arrive at an uneasy truce or come to the conclusion that the marriage isn't going to work? Again, you decide.

If you feel that the guidance and exercises in this section have given you a fuller understanding of the way dialogue functions, this might be a good moment to pause and think about a writing project you are currently working on, asking yourself whether you might improve it by a more extensive or more sharply focused use of dialogue.

– 5 –
Point of view

Definitions

Let's begin by defining point of view and considering its significance in the context of our writing. Point of view is the position from which we perceive a subject. In early usage the phrase implied the *physical* position of the observer in relation to a concrete subject (a point of view was typically the place from which a fine building or picturesque landscape might be observed to greatest advantage) but it quickly took on figurative overtones, implying a *mental* position or attitude (as in 'From my point of view it seems obvious that war solves nothing, though I appreciate that others may see the matter differently'). As writers of fiction we need to consider both meanings of the phrase.

Although 'point of view' is the term you're most likely to come across in creative writing handbooks, you might also like to consider the phrase 'centre of consciousness' which, because it avoids privileging the sense of sight (implicit in 'view'), usefully steers us towards a broader understanding of narrative perspective. The phrase allows for the registering of all sensual experience that falls within the narrator's range, as well as for the narrator's interpretation of what is registered.

Most readers of this book will know what is meant by the terms 'first-person' and 'third-person' in relation to narrative, but since they are central to any discussion of point of view, it may be helpful to remind ourselves of their meaning. A first-person narrative is a story told in the voice of a character who is always in some sense party to the events the narrative describes and is usually the central character. A third-person narrative operates at a greater distance from the events described; the narrator – best imagined as a disembodied voice – communicates the thoughts and actions of the fictional characters but plays no active part in their story. You may be tempted to think of this disembodied voice as the voice of the author, and that's understandable, though modern critical discourse rightly insists on a distinction between author and narrator, whether or not the distinction is apparent in the writing itself.

That's it in a nutshell, but as we explore these matters in the exercises that follow we shall inevitably be constructing a broader and more complex picture. This will be particularly evident in relation to the range of options offered by a third-person narrative; but let's begin our explorations by examining a passage written in the first person.

First-person viewpoint

Remembering what my father used to say about the importance of first impressions, I swept my hair back from my face and drew myself up to my full height. I knocked at the door, a smart rat-a-tat. I wanted Miss Driscoll to know I meant business.

No answer. I waited a moment, then knocked again, holding my breath, listening. A door opened somewhere towards the back of the house and I heard music – the radio, I imagined – and then footsteps coming towards me, clicking sharply on tiles or flagstones.

'Who is it?'

A man's voice; not what I'd been expecting.

'I'm Camille. Is Miss Driscoll there?'

The door opened and a face peered out, sallow and unshaven. The man looked me up and down. I thought I heard a movement in the hallway behind him but couldn't be certain.

'She's not here.'

By the time you get to the end of the opening sentence of this passage you'll already have picked up on the obvious indicators: 'I', 'my' and 'myself' immediately define this as a first-person narrative. You'll notice, too, the inwardness of the passage – the sense it gives us of sharing not only what Camille hears and sees, but also what she remembers, imagines or expects.

This inwardness is one of the great advantages of the first-person viewpoint, but it has a corresponding disadvantage: the intimate perspective allows us, as writers, to dig deeply into the mind of our narrator, but it's also likely to restrict our exploration of the mental processes of other characters. More than that, it limits or complicates our coverage of the action: events that are not witnessed by the narrator must enter the narrative indirectly, from other sources – in dialogue or reported speech, in letters received or journal entries conveniently discovered. This isn't, of course, an argument against using the first-person viewpoint, but an argument for establishing, preferably from an early stage in your writing of any given work of fiction, what narrative viewpoint will best serve its particular needs.

In the passage above you'll notice that Camille's physical position, on the wrong side of a closed door, prevents her from establishing with certainty the source of the music she hears: the phrase 'the radio, *I imagined*' keeps subtly in play the possibility of another source – a record player, for example; and, hearing footsteps on a hard surface but unable to see what that surface is, she considers two alternative possibilities: 'tiles or flagstones'. She is also uncertain whether or not she has detected a movement in an unseen part of the hallway. In recognising the limits of her knowledge (from her standpoint at that particular moment) the narrative ties us firmly to Camille's point of view.

With all this in mind, let's move on to the first exercise.

1.
Imagine yourself on the other side of the closed door. You're the unshaven, sallow-faced man – let's call him Charlie – who hears Camille's knock and eventually answers it. Is Miss Driscoll in the house? If she is, does a brief conversation take place before

Charlie goes to the door? Does he have to prepare himself in any way to meet the (to him) unknown caller? What's going on in his mind as he moves down the hallway? It's up to you to invent the details, but the basic task is to write a first-person narrative from Charlie's point of view. As you develop the narrative, you'll be thinking both about what he knows and what (from his particular viewpoint) he can't know.

Looking over the piece you've written you'll probably see that, although you've been dealing with the same incident, the change of viewpoint has produced a narrative very different from the one in which Camille was the centre of consciousness. When we begin to write a first-person narrative we usually have an intuitive sense of the viewpoint that allows us to tell our story most fully and most forcefully, but it can sometimes be helpful to audition other characters for the narrative 'I', even if only to rule them out.

Third-person viewpoints

In daily life the first person tends to dominate our discourse. The reason is obvious: each of us is the centre of consciousness in our own lives, and our day-to-day narratives reflect this. A parent asks a child what happened at school during the day, or a husband asks a wife what the office party was like, and even though others are involved, the ensuing narratives will naturally default to the first person.

While first-person narratives are by no means rare in fiction, it's probably fair to say that the default mode in novels and short stories is the third person; it's certainly the case that third person is more common than first person. Third-person narratives may adopt a position very close to a character (tight third person) or may operate from a greater distance; the tendency of the fiction of the past hundred years or so towards tighter positioning reflects a wider cultural shift, with greater weight being given more generally to inward experience and subjective judgement. We might reasonably consider the tight third person to be the dominant mode in contemporary fiction, and there's a strong chance that, looking back over your own writing, you'll find that most of it falls into this category.

Reverting to Camille as the centre of consciousness, we'll now reset the narrative in tight third person. This can be done very simply, with a change of pronouns:

> *Remembering what her father used to say about the importance of first impressions, she swept her hair back from her face and drew herself up to her full height. She knocked at the door, a smart rat-a-tat. She wanted Miss Driscoll to know she meant business…*

And so on. If that's all we're doing, it might not seem to matter whether we choose the first person or the third: the narrative remains restricted to Camille's perspective. But the choice would matter if we wanted the freedom to shift the centre of consciousness from one character to another, as here:

> *The door opened and a face peered out, sallow and unshaven. The man looked her up and down. She thought she heard a movement in the hallway behind him but couldn't be certain.*
>
> 'She's not here.'
>
> *It's her, he thought. It must be. Eyes like her mother's, the same upright bearing. He felt his heart hammering at his ribs and wondered fleetingly whether the shock might kill him. He had imagined this moment so often. Now she was here, standing on his doorstep, and he had no idea what to say to her.*

Novels exist in which a number of different first-person narratives are grouped together, with the shift from one to another generally indicated by a visible break in the text (a double space or a new chapter heading). These novels may work effectively as a means of conveying a variety of responses to the same event, as well as allowing access to a wider range of events than would have been available to a single observer, but they can sometimes convey an impression of disjointedness. The passage above suggests

5 Point of view

the more fluid movement between intimately realised centres of consciousness that the choice of third person can allow. You'll appreciate that while Camille could conceivably see signs of Charlie's state of mind – he might tremble or clutch at the doorjamb – the detail of his thoughts and feelings wouldn't be known to her and therefore couldn't be conveyed to the reader from her viewpoint. If we want to show what Charlie is thinking and feeling we can shift the viewpoint without breaking the narrative flow: the use of a close but fluid third-person narrative – sometimes characterised as 'free indirect discourse' – provides much of the intimacy we associate with first-person narratives while allowing us to move freely from one centre of consciousness to another.

It's worth noting at this point that writers have to work for their freedoms. If you want to carry your readers with you – as you should – you can't simply bumble at random from one centre of consciousness to another. Even the relatively straightforward shift in the example above would be unlikely to work effectively if it came towards the end of a novel that had otherwise been written entirely from Camille's point of view. The writer has considerable leeway in establishing the terms of any given work of fiction but, once established, those terms function as an implicit contract. Writers who break that contract may lose the trust of their readers.

If you want to see a more extended (and masterly) example of the way a fluid third-person narrative can be made to work, take a look at the opening of Chapter 17 in the first section of Virginia Woolf's *To the Lighthouse*, where we move, in the space of a few pages, from Mrs Ramsay's viewpoint to Lily Briscoe's and then to Charles Tansley's, before reverting to Lily's. Though not essential, this reading would be excellent preparation for the exercise that follows.

2.
> **As in the chapter in *To the Lighthouse*, the scene is a dinner party. The hosts are Arif and his wife, Helen. Among the guests**

are Angela and her husband, Tony. Arif is Tony's boss, and this is the first time Tony and Angela have been invited to the house. Angela is nervous; Tony is anxious to impress but is distracted by Helen's remarkable beauty. Helen is keen for the party to be a success but is preoccupied by thoughts of her son, Karim, who has gone out with friends and should have been home an hour ago.

You may of course modify these details – we've provided them to assist you in the task, not to constrain you. The important point is that you'll be writing a close but fluid third-person narrative which will allow the reader to experience the situation from the viewpoint of at least two of the characters; more ambitiously, you may want to introduce three viewpoints, or even all four.

The principle isn't difficult to grasp, but the practice can be demanding. If, in reading the piece you've written, you feel that the transition between viewpoints hasn't been as fluent as you'd have liked, don't let that worry you: as with any of the exercises in this book, repeated practice will bring improvement.

In considering types of third-person narrative it's more helpful to think in terms of tendency than of sharp differentiation. If we turn now to the point of view often referred to as omniscient third person, we can say that it's a narratorial position that tends to take a more detached view of events and characters than the tight third person and that it works well for narratives that benefit from a wide focus. Consider this:

> *The guns thundered; shells battered the trenches. A thick pall of smoke hung over the battlefield, blotting the sun. There were shouted orders, calls for stretchers, cries of pain. It was more than three hours since the engagement had begun, and neither side could be said to have the advantage.*

The term 'omniscient narrative' might reasonably be applied to the passage above, but now consider this:

> *The enemy had located the gunners' position and shells were falling close at hand. The sunlight barely filtered through the pall of smoke that hung over*

the battlefield. Men were shouting, but their words were lost in the barrage of sound. There seemed no end to the bombardment, nor any purpose in it.

There's clearly a degree of distance here and, relative to the first- and tight third-person examples we looked at earlier, the field of vision is broad. But it's noticeably less broad than that of the immediately preceding passage. The centre of consciousness is now located on one particular side of the conflict rather than above the fray – '*the enemy* had located the gunners' position' – and the shells, falling 'close at hand', also suggest a more specific viewpoint. The narrator of this passage is unable to hear the words that might allow him to identify different kinds of utterance, and the phrase 'there seemed no end to' has a more subjective quality than 'it was more than three hours since' in the preceding example.

How, then, would we categorise the second of these two examples? Perhaps we should take a step back and ask ourselves whether, rather than aiming for neat categorisation, it might be helpful to view third-person narratives as occupying different points along a spectrum, points that might well vary even in the course of a single narrative – as, for example, if we were to follow 'nor any purpose in it' in the passage above with this sentence: 'Matthew huddled back against the trench wall, terror-stricken, hoping no-one would notice him.' This would lead us naturally into tight third-person territory, recalibrating the viewpoint without deranging the narrative.

Categories are useful to us as writers: without them we would find it difficult to explain the intricacies of our craft to others or get a grip on them for our own creative purposes. But we need to recognise the organic nature of good fiction writing, its resistance to schematic representation. In the present context this means acknowledging that the centre of consciousness in a third-person narrative may not be rigidly fixed, and that a degree of fluidity, properly understood and handled, may work to our advantage.

So for the next exercise we're not going to ask you to strive for an ideal and perhaps unattainable omniscience, but simply to represent an event from a point of view which, if not entirely unlocated, is detached from any particular character.

3.
Describe an event involving a significant number of people, aiming for a broad perspective. This doesn't mean that you can't home in on detail, but that, for present purposes, you should avoid viewpoints closely tied to one or other of the individuals involved. You may want to choose your own subject, or you may prefer to base your piece on one of the following:

a) a football match

b) an earthquake

c) a music festival

d) a fight in a pub

If you choose an event outside your own experience, remember that newspaper reports can be a valuable source of information; some may also function as a useful model for the relatively distant or largely detached viewpoint recommended for this exercise, though you should bear in mind that a good fiction writer usually aims at something more complex than mere reportage.

Reflecting on this exercise, you may feel that maintaining the recommended narrative distance was more difficult than you'd anticipated. Since, as noted earlier, twentieth- and twenty-first-century fiction has tended towards greater inwardness than the fiction of earlier periods, we're naturally likely, both as readers and writers, to favour more intimate viewpoints. If you gravitated at times towards tighter versions of third-person narrative, that's no problem as long as you recognise the fact: the point of the exercises in this section is simply to give you a stronger sense of the range of narrative viewpoints available to you and to provide the kind of practice in using them that will lead to deeper understanding and greater control.

Unreliable narratives

An unreliable narrative is a narrative whose view of the world is questionable – not merely in the sense that some readers may not share the narrator's beliefs, but in the sense that all readers are actively invited to doubt them. An extreme example is Edgar Allan Poe's famous short story 'The Tell-Tale Heart', a tale of murder told by a narrator who begins by attempting to establish his credibility; he seems to believe he is sane but the more frantically he presses the point, the crazier he seems to the reader. More subtly, Stevens in Kazuo Ishiguro's *The Remains of the Day* (1989) and, more recently, Eleanor in *Eleanor Oliphant is Completely Fine* (2018) by Gail Honeyman, both lag well behind the attentive reader in their understanding of the stories they tell, even though they are centrally involved in the events chronicled.

Look at this example of unreliable narration, considering the way it gradually undermines its own opening statement:

> *Loretta was the one who broke up the marriage. She was a difficult woman, demanding and controlling. Always wanting to know where I was, who I was with, what I was doing. It was like living under a curfew – if I came in any time after midnight there'd be recriminations, and on the rare occasions I spent the night somewhere else there'd be hell to pay. And she'd poke her nose in where she had no business, calling my ex-girlfriends to ask where I was, even though they were hardly ever in a position to know – you could count on the fingers of one hand the times I was actually with one of them when she phoned. Unreasonable behaviour, I'd call it, and I told her as much when she walked out on me, taking the kids with her.*

An egotistical attempt at self-justification, this is a narrative whose explicitly stated premise – that Loretta was responsible for the marital break-up – is implicitly challenged at every turn. Whose behaviour, we are tacitly invited to ask, is really unreasonable – the wife's or the narrator's? And while views of sexual morality are admittedly variable, it's a fair bet that you'll have read the passage not as self-justification but as self-indictment, an apparently inadvertent confession by a narrator who may have deceived himself but is unlikely to deceive many of his readers.

Even if you never go on to write a more extended unreliable narrative, immersion in one or more of the following exercises will be useful, helping you towards a general understanding of the relationship between text (what is explicitly stated) and subtext (what is suggested). Here, the text and the subtext will be sharply at odds with one another, setting up an interesting tension in the narrative.

4.
- a) Write a passage of first-person narrative from the point of view of someone who has joined a cult. In describing its rules and rituals, he reveals their absurdity or oppressiveness – and his own gullibility – even as he explicitly promotes the view that the cult holds the secret of human happiness.

- b) Write a passage of first-person narrative from the point of view of someone who considers herself to be plagued by inconsiderate neighbours. Allow the narrative to reveal, as it continues, that the bad neighbour is the narrator herself – that she is, without seeing it, the real source of the problem.

- c) Write a passage of first-person narrative from the point of view of someone who considers himself to be the victim of bullying in his workplace. Allow the narrative to reveal, as it continues, that his difficulties with his fellow workers are actually the result of his own bullying behaviour.

- d) Write a passage of first-person narrative from the point of view of someone who considers her life to have been a failure. Allow the narrative to reveal, as it describes her supposed failures,

5 Point of view

that she has actually been a high-achiever in one or more spheres of life.

As you addressed these exercises you were probably conscious not only of what your narrators were saying but also of the manner in which they said it. Any discussion of narrative viewpoint is likely to touch, sooner or later, on the subject of narrative voice, which is the focus of our next section.

– 6 –

Narrative voice

Definitions

A work of fiction will usually contain many voices, most of them represented in dialogue; these are the voices of its characters. But when we talk about narrative voice we're speaking of the overarching voice, the voice that tells the story. As you might expect, there are cases that complicate the matter. In Section 5 we mentioned first-person narratives presented from a number of different viewpoints; this variety of viewpoint may be matched by a variety of distinct voices, and in such cases it would be misleading to speak of an overarching voice. Even so, the fact remains that most novels and short stories are dominated by a single (though not necessarily unmodulated) voice, the primary source of the reader's knowledge of the events of the narrative.

Narrative voice in first-person narratives

Writers who opt for a first-person viewpoint will often take advantage of the opportunity it offers to establish and explore a distinctive narrative voice. Such narratives may well provide explicit information about the narrator – about her background, her character, her world-view, her relationship to other characters – but this section is concerned less with what is said than with how it is said – with the quality, or qualities, of the voice itself. Compare these two passages:

a) *What's done is done and I don't regret it. Why should I? You get one shot at life and that's it. Shot's the word. A bullet in the back of the head. Him or me, I thought, and it was him that copped it. Maybe I was lucky, or maybe too smart for him – whatever, I'm still on my feet and he's six feet under.*

6 Narrative voice

b) When I consider the way the drama played out, I realise that everything had to happen as it did. I've no reason to regret the outcome, since the alternative is unthinkable: if I hadn't pulled the trigger when I did he would certainly have taken advantage of my hesitation. It's possible that luck played a part – suppose he had turned as I crept up behind him? – but it's equally possible that it was my native wit that saved me. However you look at it, the fact remains that he's gone and I'm here to tell the story.

You'll see at once that, while the passages cover more or less the same narrative ground, the difference between the two voices significantly affects our reading – in particular our perception of the narrators. We might reasonably suppose from the punchy, colloquial discourse that the narrator of example a) is less well educated than the narrator of b) and more straightforward in his thinking; more subtly, we might observe that, while both narrators seem reluctant to engage with the enormity of their actions, their approaches are different – briskly dismissive in the case of narrator a) and delicately evasive in the case of narrator b).

The following exercise will give you an opportunity to experiment along similar lines.

1.

Imagine two sharply differentiated characters. One is practical and courageous, not much given to reflection; the other is timid, uncertain, and reflective to the point at which even minor decisions are difficult. The first character has persuaded the second to join her on a hiking expedition in a remote mountainous region. Two days into their journey it becomes apparent to both of them that they are lost.

What happens in your narrative is for you to decide, but the same episode should be narrated twice, once in the voice of each character. For the purposes of the exercise it would be best not to stray into dialogue, but to keep the focus firmly on the voice that tells the story.

Looking back on this exercise you'll realise that the experience undergone by the two narrators is essentially the same; the differences in narrative voice arise from differences of character. In the following exercise difference is heightened by the fact that, although the two characters share the event, they occupy very different positions in relation to it, and their voices are further differentiated by age: the fact that one is an adult and the other a child will affect your response to the exercise.

2.

> The scene is a dental surgery. A ten-year-old child is sitting in the dentist's chair undergoing treatment at the hands of a young dentist who is both nervous and taciturn; he gives the impression of being unused to dealing with children. This is the first time the child has needed treatment and her father is sitting in with her, increasingly anxious as the treatment progresses. Narrate the episode firstly from the father's point of view and in his voice; then switch narrators, as in the previous exercise, so that it is the child's experience we share, the child's voice we hear. Again, you'll get the most out of this exercise if you keep the focus on the narrative voice, avoiding dialogue.

As you tackled this exercise you may have found the rendering of the child's voice particularly challenging. In order to make the narrative convincing you will have had to consider carefully the likely limitations of the voice – a fairly restricted vocabulary and a plausibly unsophisticated syntax. Having considered these matters, however, you have probably settled on a point somewhere between the typical speech patterns of a ten-year-old and those of a literate adult; if so, this is probably right. What the writer is aiming for in such cases isn't usually the mere imitation of a voice less sophisticated than his own, but an impressionistic suggestion of it.

You'll find a good example of this delicate balancing act in Peter Carey's *True History of the Kelly Gang*, in which the limitations of the poorly educated narrator are represented by very rudimentary punctuation. We know, of course, that other indications of inadequate schooling – misspellings, inappropriate word choices and grammatical confusions – would normally, in real life, be part of the picture, but we are invited to buy into the convention established from the outset by the author; to accept one key aspect of unsophisticated discourse as indicative of a wider inadequacy. It's a strategy that allows Carey to represent his narrator's limitations without inhibiting his own authorial reach.

Balancing acts of a broadly similar nature play a part in a variety of first-person narratives. Any thoughtful writer of historical fiction is likely to be making linguistic choices which, to a greater or lesser extent, reflect the discourse of the period in which the work is set, while at the same time keeping the contemporary reader on board; and a writer who renders a narrative in a regional dialect of English will possibly (though not necessarily) want to temper authenticity with a concern to speak to an inclusive readership – not only to readers familiar with the dialect in question but also to those who have to learn how to read it.

Let's take historical fiction first. The writer will need to navigate between mere pastiche or mimicry on the one hand and, on the other, a flagrant disregard for the history of the English language. Hilary Mantel favours 'an idiom that has a suggestion of the era rather than trying to imitate it slavishly', and although this middle ground can't be clearly demarcated, most serious works of historical fiction occupy some portion of it.

You may find it helpful to take two runs at the next exercise. Your first draft will establish a narrative voice broadly appropriate to the specified historical period; your second draft will involve research and fine-tuning as you pick up on words and phrases that might be historically questionable, checking and editing as appropriate. And there's more to it than that: there are questions to be asked about style. To what extent do you want your own work to reflect the narrative style of an age generally more attuned to longer and more elaborate sentence structures than our own? Can you acknowledge these structures without simply aping them? Can you, in other words, create a narrative voice that both honours the past and speaks vibrantly to the present?

3.

It's 1840. A young woman has been sent away by her parents, in the hope that distance will put an end to her infatuation with a young man who lives close to her home, and whom they consider to be an inappropriate match; she is to spend a year in an ugly industrial city with a strict maiden aunt whom she detests.

Shortly after her arrival she shuts herself in her room and composes a letter to the young man, describing her journey and her new circumstances. Your task is to write that letter in a voice at once lively and broadly appropriate to the period. Other characters may figure in the woman's narrative – her fellow travellers on the journey, her aunt – but for the purposes of the exercise it would, once again, be best to avoid dialogue.

In addressing the exercise you'll no doubt have considered the available means of transport; you may also have thought about contemporary manners and fashions. Matters of this kind are important, and will be touched on in Section 10, but our primary focus in the present context is on language. There are no firm rules here, but your intuition – perhaps supported by a glance at the relevant entries in the *Oxford English Dictionary*, which is your most reliable guide to historical usage – may suggest the inappropriateness of (for example) having your narrator describe one of her fellow travellers as 'a total nutter' or having her sign herself 'Your loving girlfriend'. As Mantel suggests, we must allow ourselves some flexibility in these matters, but the serious writer of historical fiction will want to avoid glaring anachronisms – terms and usages that risk jolting the reader out of the narrative's historical period. This applies most obviously to first-person narratives, where the narrator usually occupies the same time-frame as the characters whose lives are described, but even in the case of an omniscient third-person narrative there's a strong argument for a style concordant with the period setting.

And so to the problematic matter of rendering dialect and accent in narrative voice. When the novelist Sam Selvon began writing his 1956 novel *The Lonely Londoners*, he used the dialect of his native Trinidad for the dialogue but initially chose what he referred to as 'straight English' for the narrative voice. It wasn't until he decided also to set the narrative in dialect that, as he described it, 'the novel just shot along'.

It's an instructive example. Selvon needed to find the right voice for his narrative, but the important point is that he didn't have to look very far: the voice he chose was one with which he was intimately familiar by reason of his background and upbringing. Before you approach the following exercise, consider how well placed you are to render a narrative in a voice reflective of one of the many regional dialects of English. Note that Selvon freed himself into a dialect that came naturally to him; if, in your own case, no regional dialect comes naturally, it would probably be wise simply to acknowledge this and skip the exercise.

Yet the exercise is here for a good reason: many aspiring writers have come to share with Selvon that profound sense of liberation when a voice they may have stifled, or considered inappropriate in a literary context, is given its due in their writing. If you feel that this exercise will help you bring to the fore a dialect with which you are familiar, try it now.

4.
Write a brief first-person narrative in your chosen voice. It may help to take as your starting point an incident from your own life, though you should feel free to fictionalise in whatever ways best serve the narrative's needs. You may also find it helpful in this instance to use dialogue as a means of re-accessing or reinforcing the chosen voice, though for the purposes of the exercise your primary focus will still be the voice in which the narrative is set.

Even as you were writing you may have registered complications. Voice varies not only according to region but also according to character and social background, and these matters will affect your choices. Marlon James's *A Brief History of Seven Killings* is set in Jamaica and the majority of its various first-person narrative voices are rendered in the dialect of the region, but not identically so: a woman who has been employed as a receptionist tells her story in a voice recognisably Jamaican but noticeably closer to standard English than the voices of the local gang members. Whether or not you ever want to write a multi-stranded narrative of this kind, it will be helpful to consider James's nuanced approach to regional dialect. You may also have identified complications connected with the marketability and potential breadth of readership, but those aren't our concerns here; the important thing at this stage is simply to use your knowledge of a particular dialect to create a lively and compelling narrative.

Narrative voice in third-person narratives

Writing in the first person will give you greater opportunities to explore a distinctive narrative voice than writing in the third person; obviously, however, all narratives have a voice, and all writers need to consider the nature of that voice. The fundamental question of whether your narrative leans towards tight third person or a broader viewpoint is a choice with implications for the narrative voice, while other matters, of a more specific nature, must also be considered. For example, historical narratives written in the third person will still usually need to be (within the parameters discussed above in relation to first-person narratives) period-appropriate, while a hard-hitting urban thriller is unlikely to be written in the same voice as a tale of an idyllic childhood spent in an isolated rural community.

Most writers tend, as they develop, to gravitate towards the kinds of writing that come most readily to them, and towards the narrative voices that best serve their creative purposes, but versatility is a strength, and early-stage writers in particular would be well advised to explore a range of voices. At the beginning of this section we noted in passing that the overarching voice of a narrative isn't

6 Narrative voice

necessarily unmodulated, and practice in handling tonal shifts will help you to avoid monotony in any given work of fiction; it will also allow you greater freedom to experiment with a range of genres.

The following exercise asks you to write in the third person, but much of what we've said about first-person narrative voice is also applicable here.

5.

In a battle in the Crimean War of 1853–1856, a young British soldier is wounded but escapes from the battlefield. Feverish and confused, he goes into hiding in the woods adjacent to a small village. He is discovered by a young woman, who brings him food and tends his wounds. Your task is to write two brief sections of narrative, both in the third person: the first will be an account of the battle, fought brutally and at close quarters; the second will deal with the developing relationship between the soldier and the woman who is nursing him. Neither character speaks the other's language, so there is no dialogue.

You may need to do a little research here – it might, for example, prove difficult to write about a mid nineteenth-century battle without knowing something about the kinds of weapon used at the time – but for present purposes it would be best to restrict your research to such details as your narrative actually needs: your primary focus is the narrative voice and the ways in which this voice might vary according to the nature of the scenes described. Be aware, in your writing, of the mood you want to convey; and keep in view the value of a discourse that is broadly appropriate to the period in question.

The exercise has been designed to give you considerable freedom with regard both to the narrative itself and the manner in which you convey it, but the chances are that you'll observe a significant tonal shift between your first passage and your second – a reminder that what we call narrative voice may actually be a series of voices, modulated in such a way as to serve, collectively, the complex and varied needs of your fiction.

– 7 –
Beginnings and endings

~

'Begin at the beginning,' says the King to the White Rabbit in Lewis Carroll's *Alice in Wonderland*, 'and go on till you come to the end; then stop.' As readers, we might regard the instruction as straightforward to the point of redundancy; as writers, however, we'll be aware that the question of where (and how) a story begins and ends is a complex one, demanding careful thought. The exercises in this section are designed to assist you in your thinking and to help you explore the range of possibilities available to you.

Beginnings

The opening of a novel or short story may perform many functions, but above all it has to engage its readers. Imagine those readers standing on the threshold of your fictional world, wondering whether to enter, and then ask yourself how you might persuade them to do so. What kinds of approach might draw them in?

An obvious way of providing the hook you need is to open your narrative with a slice of high-octane action. There are important caveats, and we'll come to these shortly, but for the moment just see how you get on with the following exercise.

1.
> In 1847, at the height of the Great Famine, a young Irishman leaves his parents' home with the intention of making a better life for himself in America. He has never been to sea before, and knows nothing of seafaring life. On the outward voyage the sailing ship in which he is travelling is blown off course and wrecked. Taking these bare details as your starting point and developing

7 Beginnings and endings

them in any way you wish, write an opening that will draw readers into your narrative and make them eager to read more.

Many good works of fiction begin with a compelling action scene of the kind suggested by this prompt, and the contemporary demand for such openings is strong: some literary agents and editors will push writers firmly in this direction. There is, however, a danger in an over-heavy or exclusive emphasis on this relatively straightforward form of hook: writers who are prevented from experimenting with subtler (and perhaps deeper) ways of engaging their readers may find themselves working against the grain of their own particular interests and talents. You'll almost certainly have learned useful lessons from the exercise you've just completed, but it won't have given you an all-purpose template.

One of the matters you'll have had to consider in responding to the prompt is your point of entry into the narrative. Look at these two opening sentences, both drawing on the prompt above but entering at very different points:

a) *In the spring of 1847, with no sign of an end to the famine that was then afflicting the country of my birth, I resolved to take ship for America and, with that end in view, set off on foot for Dublin.*

b) *I woke in darkness to the creak and crash of splintering wood, the sailors' cries and the pounding of feet on the deck above.*

We shouldn't dismiss the first of these two sentences out of hand – after all, it economically provides a considerable amount of contextual information, much of which may ultimately be important to the narrative – but we might reasonably observe that the second sentence, hurling us directly into the drama of the shipwreck, offers a stronger and more immediate hook.

Developing writers have a tendency to begin their stories at an earlier stage of the plot than is strictly necessary, front-loading expository material that might better be drip-fed into their narrative as it proceeds. If you think this may apply to you, you might like to return now to the opening passage you've just written, weighing up the advantages – and possible disadvantages – of starting later in the sequence of events.

Opening with a passage of dramatic action can be an extremely effective strategy, but you'll probably realise that if this were the only way of gaining the attention of readers, many famous works of fiction would have gone unread. What else might provide a good point of entry to your narrative?

We've spoken earlier about the importance of character, and you might perhaps choose to open with some account of your protagonist's views and feelings. Your challenge in such a case is to find a source of energy in the relevant details – something, for example, in your character's expression or demeanour that hints at internal conflict, or a suggestion that the character isn't quite what she appears to be. You might consider the value of providing another character as interlocutor, allowing your protagonist's character to emerge through lively dialogue as well as through description. Then again, you might want to foreground the story's physical setting in your opening, perhaps describing a house, a city street or a rural landscape – evoking atmosphere, establishing contextual details that will help readers to understand the environment in which your characters' lives are patterned out.

Character and location are not, of course, mutually exclusive alternatives, and the next exercise invites you to work with both.

2.

Two brothers, James and John, are having a drink together in a wine bar when a casual remark from James gives John a piece of information about their family's history – an important matter of which John has previously been unaware. Your task is to create an opening which, without using dramatic physical action as the hook, will nevertheless engage your readers' attention from the outset. Write the passage in such a way as to reveal the characters of the two brothers, perhaps accentuating the differences between them, while at the same time giving a strong sense of

their surroundings. For example, is the bar's atmosphere homely or soulless? Is it conducive to conversation or are there repeated interruptions?

You'll need to consider the nature of James's revelation, but bear in mind that it's not the job of an opening to explain everything at once; indeed, a degree of reticence, suggestive of further revelations to come, may play a part in persuading your readers to read on.

In asking you to write an opening that doesn't rely on dramatic action as a means of engaging your readers we are, of course, creating an artificial restriction. The idea behind this particular exercise is to focus your attention on matters that might easily be overlooked in your search for an arresting opening for your narrative; but when we noted, in introducing the exercise, that character and location are not mutually exclusive alternatives, we might have added that neither of them precludes the possibility of beginning with a scene of dramatic action. The next exercise will invite you to work with all three elements, drawing them together in a single narrative with the aim of creating a rich and densely textured opening. By way of example, let's revisit the shipboard scene of exercise 1, building on the second of the two opening sentences provided there:

> *I woke in darkness to the creak and crash of splintering wood, the sailors' cries and the pounding of feet on the deck above. Strange, I thought, but from the time I had come on board everything had seemed strange to me, and for a moment I was able to convince myself that whatever was happening was part of the pattern of things in this alien world of wind and water. Then the ship lurched wildly and I was thrown sidelong from my berth.*
>
> *My fellow passengers were struggling to their feet; the clamour above grew louder. I recognised the panic in the sailors' voices and realised, with something approaching terror, that my confidence in their skills and experience had been misplaced: they were no match for the raging sea. I scuttled crabwise to the ladder, climbed it and pushed open the hatch. If I was to be drowned it wouldn't be below decks in my cramped and crowded quarters, boxed in like a trapped rat, but out in the wind and the drenching spray.*

Dramatic action may be foregrounded here, but the context of the action is also made clear, as are the character's shifting emotions as he grapples with new experiences in an unfamiliar world. With the example in mind, try the following exercise.

3.
A young woman is walking through a city at dusk when she hears the sounds of a violent disturbance coming from a basement flat. She has just phoned the police when a man rushes out with a knife in his hand and runs away up the street. Hoping to keep tabs on him, she follows at what she thinks is a safe distance, but as they cross a stretch of wasteland he looks back and sees her. He starts to run towards her.

Taking these details as the basis for your narrative, write an opening that engages the reader through the vivid representation of action, character and location. The action has been partially mapped out for you, and the scene has been broadly set – though in both cases you should feel free to adapt as you see fit, and you'll certainly need to expand on the details provided. The character and feelings of the woman are undefined in the passage above, and you'll need to decide for yourself who she is. It matters, of course: if, for example, she is a highly trained former army officer your narrative is likely to be very different from one in which she is a naive young student addicted to crime fiction.

When you've finished, look back over the work you've produced. The hope is that you've created something worthwhile and that you've learned from the process, but if you also feel a little less than satisfied with the piece, this shouldn't surprise or discourage you: gathering all this diverse material into an opening at once coherent, compelling and appropriately complex is no easy task. Here, as elsewhere, you may have found it relatively straightforward to establish the intended content of your narrative, but beyond that there's always the more difficult challenge of fashioning the words to frame that content.

And this brings us to a final but centrally important point about openings: however you choose to start your story, it's worth remembering that the quality of your writing may itself function as an effective hook. Stylistic fluency, an original and vivid image, an apt but arresting word choice, a well-turned phrase, a finely cadenced sentence – any or all of these may serve to draw your readers into your fictional world.

Endings

Many stories have clear-cut endings, often determined by the completion of a more or less predictable narrative arc: the hero and heroine marry, the villain gets his come-uppance, a family is reunited; or, particularly in short fiction, we may encounter a twist or punchline that brings the narrative to an emphatic close. Stories of this kind may serve as useful models for our writing, but it's worth remembering that a significant proportion of modernist and contemporary literary fiction shows a marked resistance to closure of this kind.

'Life', wrote D. H. Lawrence in his essay 'The Poetry of the Present', 'knows no finality, no finished crystallisation'; and while our fictional representations of life must necessarily at some point be brought to a conclusion, Lawrence was clearly pushing against this constraint when he concluded *Women in Love* in the middle of an argument between his two protagonists, implicitly encouraging the reader to imagine the conversation continuing beyond the point at which the text itself comes to an end. Along with his contemporaries James Joyce, Virginia Woolf and Katherine Mansfield, Lawrence helped to establish as a literary norm a far greater open-endedness than we typically find in the works of his nineteenth-century predecessors.

As we've suggested in other contexts, writing requires us not to make simple binary choices – in this case, open ending or closed – but to find an appropriate point on a spectrum of possibilities. You might, for example, consider it appropriate to conclude a crime story with a chapter in which the detective in charge of the case explains how the crime was committed and identifies the perpetrator; alternatively, you might exploit the uncertainties that conventionally precede the resolution of this kind of narrative, concluding with a suggestion that the detective has got it wrong and that the perpetrator will go unpunished while an innocent man is jailed; or you might end on a note of existential anxiety, with the detective cleverly solving the case but walking out into the night with a heightened sense of the futility of his own small successes in the face of human evil. Any of these conclusions might work for you and for your story, but you'll appreciate that they offer differing degrees of resolution.

With this in mind, let's move on to the next group of prompts.

4.

> In broad outline, the plot concerns a woman, Eileen, who befriends a fellow worker, Ewan, in the office in which she is employed. He is ten years younger than she is and popular with the younger office staff, but he seems to prefer her company to theirs. Previous experience has left her with little hope of finding a life partner, so when he asks her out for dinner she is surprised and initially cautious. As their relationship progresses, however, she is won over by his attentions, and when he eventually proposes marriage she accepts.
>
> A few months later he tells her he has found a new job, starting immediately. From this point on, things start to fall apart. The couple's evening meetings, previously frequent and regular, are often cancelled by Ewan at the last minute; on the rare occasions they do meet up he is evasive about the job and avoids all discussion of earlier plans to buy a house together. However, he strenuously resists Eileen's suggestion that they should end the relationship. Confused and suspicious, she starts to research his past and to follow him around unseen.
>
> What she discovers is for you to decide. Your task is to write three different conclusions to the story, each based on one of the following suggestions.

a) Late at night, after one too many cancelled meetings, Eileen goes to Ewan's flat to confront him. He sits her down and accounts for his behaviour in a way that dispels her anxieties. He opens his desk drawer and brings out his correspondence with a solicitor – details of a newly concluded house purchase. Our house, he tells her proudly, explaining that he had intended to call round early the following morning to surprise her with the news. The couple talk on into the small hours, making plans for a lifetime together.

b) The same explanations, but Eileen remains unconvinced. How did Ewan get the money for the house so quickly? Why has he carried out the negotiations without involving her? Why can't he meet her gaze when speaking to her? Maybe she doesn't actually put these questions to him, but her unease will colour your conclusion.

c) After one of their occasional meetings Eileen secretly follows Ewan back to his home, to which she has never been invited. He walks through streets she doesn't know and stops in front of a derelict house. He climbs the steps, pushes open the unlocked door and enters. After waiting a moment she follows him in. The place is a ruin, but from somewhere upstairs comes the flickering light of a candle.

What happens next? That's up to you, but in writing your conclusion consider the possibility of leaving Eileen – and your reader – with a strong sense of mystery and uncertainty.

If any of these prompts worked particularly well for you – or particularly badly – it would be worth thinking about the reasons. Some writers will welcome the certainties of prompt a) and will also, perhaps, be drawn to the happy ending it suggests, while others will see it as providing too little scope for the imagination: both as writers and as readers we may find ourselves unsatisfied by endings that neither reflect the complexities of real life nor set up reverberations that continue after the last sentence has been written, or the book closed. If you felt that either or both of the other prompts gave you greater scope and more satisfaction, this wouldn't be surprising.

If we find ourselves gravitating towards more open-ended narratives, we need to bear in mind that these require at least as much careful thought as those which come to a neater or more emphatic close. Open-endedness doesn't imply the arbitrary chopping short of a narrative but the discovery of a point of balance that simultaneously signals conclusion and denies closure. That's a fine distinction, and the process requires correspondingly fine judgement.

There's no simple recipe for a successful conclusion of this kind, but a few pointers might be helpful. Firstly, an effective conclusion is likely to consolidate the suggestions of the preceding narrative, not through mere reiteration but through amplification. Secondly, you'll find suggestion more useful than statement: a telling image, for example, is likely to work better than any explanation of a story's meaning. Thirdly, there's the cadence of the closing sentence or sentences: you can create a sense of roundedness through attention to your phrasing, bringing your narrative to an end on a note that gives the *sound* of completion, even as the *sense* of the story holds closure at bay.

We can see all of these elements in play in Raymond Carver's short story 'Everything Stuck to Him'. The plot is deceptively simple. A man meets with his grown-up daughter in Milan at Christmas time. She asks him to tell her something about her childhood and he responds with a story, told in the third person but dealing with an incident in his own life, an incident which, as he says, also involves his daughter. A young couple, he tells her, were living in a temporary home with their baby daughter. One snowy winter night the baby fell ill. The wife wanted her husband to miss a planned hunting excursion so that he could help look after the baby. He was reluctant but eventually decided to stay. His wife prepared breakfast for him. He accidentally tipped the plate into his lap, and the ensuing laughter was the prelude to a moment of reconciliation.

That, in brief, is the tale he tells, but after telling it he goes to the window and, still thinking about the incident, looks out at the snow falling over the darkened city. Carver's story ends with this sentence: 'They had leaned on each other and laughed until the tears had come, while everything else – the cold, and where he'd go in it – was outside, for a while anyway.'

The sentence sounds and feels conclusive – the text requires no addition – but it doesn't close down the reader's experience of the story. On the contrary: it accentuates the connection between the remembered incident and the narrative present and, in doing so, directs our vision outward to an uncertain future. The moment of reconciliation and laughter had been genuine but fleeting ('for a while anyway' confirms something already strongly implied in the narrative) and the phrase 'the cold, and where he'd go in it' suggests not only the journey the man has been on since the incident but also its chilly continuation beyond the present moment. And the effect is heightened by the phrase 'laughed until the tears had come': tears of laughter in the remembered moment, certainly, but the attentive reader will also pick up the secondary suggestion of laughter giving way to sorrow.

Approach the next exercise with these ideas in mind. Carver's story – which you should ideally read in its entirety – may seem a hard act to follow but you may be helped, both here and more generally, by the reflection that it's better to regard our talented predecessors as guides than as competitors.

5.
First, jot down an outline plot for a story that culminates in an epiphany – that is, a revelation or recognition of a new way of seeing things. The epiphany might be a revised understanding of a personal relationship, a suddenly heightened awareness of humankind's relationship with the natural world, a recognition of the need to come to terms with a traumatic childhood experience – or anything else that fits the bill.

Once you have a broad sense of your story, write a final paragraph that foregrounds the change of perspective and brings the narrative to a recognisable conclusion without closing it down. For example, it would almost certainly be more imaginatively fruitful to show a character grappling with the personal implications of her new environmental awareness than to show her going online and making a donation to a worthy environmental cause.

When you've finished the exercise, examine the work you've produced, asking yourself how far it reveals an expanded understanding of what might constitute a strong conclusion. You may or may not arrive at a clear answer but it's a fair bet that in addressing this and other exercises in this section you'll have developed a fuller awareness of the range of possibilities available to you, as well as a stronger sense of the kinds of beginning and ending that most closely accord with your own particular vision.

– 8 –

Pace and tension

The previous section's focus on the importance of beginnings and endings shouldn't, of course, be taken to imply the relative unimportance of all that lies between. While there's always room for debate as to where a beginning ends or an ending begins, it's clear that the remaining material will form the bulk of just about any narrative. Writing a riveting opening and a satisfying conclusion doesn't give you licence to coast through the intervening pages: every sentence you write should be as interesting as you can make it.

It's fair to acknowledge, however, that it's not always easy to maintain a high level of narrative interest. Perhaps you've had this experience: you've plotted out a number of salient points in your novel, each of which is a source of imaginative excitement for you; you may even have decided to write one or more of these episodes out of sequence, taking advantage of the creative lift your exciting material gives you. That's fine, but at some point you need to deal with the gaps you've left, and it's here that you're likely to feel your interest flagging. Where that happens the text will lose energy, and the loss of energy will then inevitably transmit itself to the reader. The exercises in this section, highlighting pace and tension, are designed to help you devise strategies for maintaining narrative energy.

In the present context, pace is the speed at which a narrative unfolds, while tension is the quality that holds the reader in a state of anticipation, eager to find out what happens next. An understanding of the way they work, both individually and in tandem, is essential to the writing of fiction.

Let's begin with a group of exercises that foreground pace.

1.
>   Using one of the following prompts as your starting point, write an account of the dramatic incident it introduces. Keep the narrative tightly focused on the action, maintaining a fast pace throughout.
>
>   a) 'Someone has to,' said Fatima, 'or the child will drown.' She kicked off her shoes and …
>
>   b) The blow seemed to come from nowhere. As Duncan fell, he …
>
>   c) With the gig only yards away Aaron darted forward, dodging the horse's hooves, and grabbed at the reins. He felt the loop snag on his fingers, but …

If you found yourself pushing the narrative forward at high speed, with tight, punchy sentences dominated by strong verbs and with dialogue (if any) kept brief and basic, that will have been an entirely appropriate response to the task you were set; but you may have realised, even as you wrote, that writing of this kind can't be sustained indefinitely. It's not simply that a narrative of any substance requires us to contextualise action – how does the action arise? who are the characters? why do they act or react as they do? – but also that keeping action at a consistently high velocity, even if it were possible, would eventually become monotonous. If, in thinking about pace, you're ever tempted to imagine that faster is necessarily better, put the idea aside. Writers need to know how to produce fast-paced writing, but they also need to know how to vary the pace, accelerating and decelerating as circumstances require.

Even the most dramatic incident will have its aftermath, and a good narrative will register the natural swell and fall of the events it describes. The next exercise invites you to reset the pace as the moment of high drama gives way to something quieter.

2.
>   Using one of the following prompts as a point of entry, write a passage dealing with the aftermath of one of the incidents from exercise 1. This could be a continuation of the passage you've already

written, or you may prefer to use one of the other prompts. The aim is to write a passage that moves at a slower and steadier *pace* than the narrative you experimented with in exercise 1 yet maintains a *tension* that will hold your reader's interest.

a) The child sat up, spat out a mouthful of water and began to cry. Fatima seated herself beside him, breathing heavily, uncertain what to do next.

b) Duncan tugged a handkerchief from his pocket and dabbed at his bloodied face. Why had he been attacked, he wondered, and who was his assailant?

c) When he had quietened the horse Aaron turned his attention to the occupant of the gig, a young woman scarcely beyond girlhood. She was sitting on the edge of the seat, her body shaking and her eyes wide in her pale face.

If, in addressing the exercise, you found ways of stepping back from the obvious excitement of the earlier dramatic event without loss of narrative energy, you will have touched on one of the secrets of good writing. Pace may be varied, but a slackening of pace should never give rise to slack writing: at every turn you face the challenge of holding your reader's attention. It's a challenge we rise to every time we reject the inert, the obvious, the unnecessary, opting instead for something that maintains narrative interest and momentum.

Whether or not you feel satisfied with your own response to the exercise, it's worth thinking generally about the ways in which writers generate momentum. We might best approach the matter by focusing on the patterning of the typical novel, with its chapter endings and headings indicating breaks in the narrative, yet also in many cases constituting an invitation to read on. What is it about a good novel that makes readers want to turn the page even as the chapter break offers them the opportunity to set the book aside?

There's no simple answer to that question, but it's fair to say that an effective chapter ending is often one that leaves the reader with a strong sense of something awaiting clarification or further development. We can illustrate this by returning to c) in the exercises above: if the young woman in the gig simply thanks Aaron for his courageous intervention and drives away we have less incentive to read on than if the chapter ends with a question, implied or explicit, that clearly needs answering. Perhaps the woman looks familiar, yet Aaron can't quite place her; perhaps she is wearing an expensive item of jewellery, inconsistent with the drabness of her clothing; perhaps she refuses to answer Aaron's well-meaning questions or tries to fob him off with obvious untruths; or perhaps the chafing on her wrists, briefly glimpsed by Aaron, suggests that she has recently been held captive. The minute you open your mind to possibilities of this kind you risk complicating your task – you might initially have wanted simply to provide evidence of Aaron's bravery or to introduce the woman he will marry at the story's conclusion – but the pay-off will almost certainly be a significantly heightened narrative tension.

So far we've discussed tension in relatively straightforward terms as a matter of plot detail withheld, with the implied promise of future revelation, but there are other factors to be taken into account by any writer looking to charge her writing with the kind of energy that makes readers eager to read on. The most significant of these is succinctness: narrative tension is dependent on the writer's fine sense of the difference between the relevant and the irrelevant, as well as on her resistance to using ten words where five will not only convey the necessary information but will do so with more style and vigour. The exercise that follows asks you to improve a rather inert narrative, refashioning it in such a way as to heighten both pace and tension.

3.
Jed has lost his dog and is sitting alone in his London bedsit when the phone rings. 'I've got a dog here', says the caller, 'an ugly brute with your number on its collar, but you're not getting

it back until you pay me. Two hundred quid should see that it comes to no harm. Finsbury Park bowling green, six o'clock. If you don't show up by then, with cash in hand, who knows what will happen?' Jed starts to say that he may need more time, but the caller has already ended the call.

The passage that follows picks up the story, but it doesn't exactly run with it. On the contrary, it's a low-energy piece that fails to take full advantage of its subject's potential, and your task is to remodel it, providing the tautness it lacks in its present form. Much of this will involve reduction and refinement – the removal of inessential material – but there's obviously material here that will need to be kept; you may also want to add material. We're not asking you to write a completely new piece; rather, we're asking you to improve on what you've been given, heightening the interest and tension of the narrative while following the contours of the original. In carrying out your improvements you'll need to decide what you wish to keep of the original text and identify what needs to be jettisoned or modified.

Jed looked at the clock on the wall. Seventeen minutes past four. That meant he had only one hour and forty-three minutes to make his way to the other side of London. He looked out of the window and saw storm clouds, dark grey but suffused at their scalloped upper edges with a deep golden light, gathering above the roof-tops and factory chimneys. It was going to rain, he thought, probably quite hard, and taking that into account along with the rush-hour traffic, he realised he might not make it in time. Should he just ignore the matter? Money was tight and the dog, a refugee from the local dogs' home, had only been with him for three weeks. In the end, though, his conscience won out and he decided he had to go.

He put on his coat and his second-best outdoor shoes and went down to the lobby. The first drops of rain were beginning to fall and it occurred to him that he should probably have worn a hat, but it was too late to do anything about that now. He hurried outside, thinking to hail a cab, but realised at once that the streets were gridlocked. He would have to take the tube.

He took his phone from his inside pocket and consulted it. He would need to change at King's Cross, where the walk between platforms through the early evening crowds would slow him down, but there was no viable alternative. He pulled up his collar against the rain and made for Goldhawk Road tube station.

He arrived at the platform to find it packed with a seething mass of impatient commuters. The train's arrival was delayed; so was its departure, due to a passenger's carelessly held umbrella getting jammed between the automatic doors. And then, less than a minute after setting off again, the train came to a standstill. Jed looked at his watch. He only had one hour and twelve minutes in hand, and his journey had barely begun.

We left it very much up to you how you approached this task, and with good reason: there's plenty of room for debate about what should be trimmed from a slack and verbose passage, and about ways in which relevance might be given to the apparently irrelevant. You might, for example, home in on the moral dilemma (does Jed fork out the ransom money for a dog he isn't particularly attached to?) and decide that it could reasonably be dispensed with – after all, nothing much is made of this detail in the text you've been given, and the problem seems to be resolved as soon as it has been raised. But if, on the other hand, you ensure that the dilemma continues to trouble Jed as he travels, raising the possibility that he might abandon his attempt to save the dog, you can significantly heighten the narrative tension.

This said, it might nevertheless be worth looking back over your piece to see how far you were able to identify and correct the weaknesses of the original. You might, for example, have asked yourself whether you needed the specificity of the various references to time ('Seventeen minutes past four. That meant he had only one hour and forty-three minutes' and so on.) It's true that the pressure of time is an essential component of the passage, but you were probably able to find more economical ways of introducing and sustaining the tension it provides.

And you'll probably have noticed that there's a more general over-provision of detail: you may have picked up on the second-best shoes, the inside pocket or the carelessly held umbrella that jams the train's doors, noting that, since these details add nothing of significance, they could be dropped without damage to the story; more than that, you probably realised that their failure to justify their place in the story meant that they *should* be dropped.

You may also have queried the presence in the text of the description of the storm clouds – 'dark grey but suffused at their scalloped upper edges with a deep golden light'. Without suggesting that all descriptive writing is an impediment to the creation of tension, we might reasonably observe that the elaborate phrase sounds a jarring note in the present context, creating an unnecessary distraction from the action. It's not only that readers will sense a slight loss of momentum but also that they may register the inappropriateness, in a tight third-person narrative, of introducing details that the character himself would be unlikely to notice in his otherwise-preoccupied state of mind. Stay with the character and his immediate concerns and you'll stand a better chance of ratcheting up the tension.

There are related considerations around such phrases as 'It was going to rain, he thought, probably quite hard, and taking that into account along with the rush-hour traffic' or 'He hurried outside, thinking to hail a cab, but realised at once that the streets were gridlocked'. Tension tends to increase with immediacy, and you'll probably be able to see now, if you hadn't already seen, how much more effective it would be to substitute ongoing action for anticipatory thought – showing Jed bursting through the lobby door to the hooting of traffic and the shouts of frustrated motorists, before making a dash for the tube station as torrential rain begins to fall. It's true that our characters may sometimes need to 'think' or 'realise', but you'll understand that immersive narrative action can often be more conducive to tension than the mental processes that precede or follow it.

Suspense: we haven't yet used the word in this discussion but you'll appreciate that what we've described as tension is often – perhaps usually – a form of suspense. To keep readers waiting for something they want to know, and to exercise good judgement in estimating the length of time they are likely to be prepared to wait, is part of the stock-in-trade of the good writer. This is obviously the case with a thriller, but suspense may operate in less dramatic ways – as, for example, in Jane Austen's *Pride and Prejudice*, where the overarching question is whether the Bennet sisters will find husbands, while the particular obstacles and uncertainties that hinder their progress towards marriage keep the reader on edge, eager to find out how each check will be negotiated.

Inexperienced writers will often miss this crucial point, pre-empting an event, discovery or realisation in such a way as to diminish the potential of their narrative. There may occasionally be a particular reason for a writer to start a story with a sentence such as 'It was on Brian's sixteenth birthday that he discovered that the man who had brought him up as his son was not, in fact, his father', but you can see how such an opening might weaken the tension of what follows. While it's admittedly possible to imagine the sentence as a doorway into an arresting narrative, it would be far more likely to function as a spoiler: the giveaway risks undermining our curiosity – the very quality required to keep us turning the pages. With this cautionary example in mind, try the following exercise.

4.
  Taking your cue from one of the following sentences, write a piece of flash fiction (up to 1,000 words) that holds back the sentence's crucial revelation until the end of the narrative. If, in the course of the exercise, you find additional means of heightening the tension of your narrative, feel free to experiment with them.

  a) I had always disliked Morgan but I never suspected that he would turn out to be the arsonist responsible for the destruction of my father's barn.

  b) The moment Annette saw the house she fell in love with it, but as a humble maidservant she could hardly have imagined that she would one day become the mistress of Harley Hall.

c) We had often mocked Darren for his obsessive interest in the old mineshafts that dotted the hills around our home town, but on one memorable occasion his knowledge saved us from disaster.

However you've approached this exercise, it's likely that you'll have come to a fuller appreciation of the value of deferment: to alert readers from the outset to the identity of a criminal or the upward trajectory of a rags-to-riches life story, or to make it clear that a potential disaster will be averted, is usually to forfeit narrative tension. Your response to the task will almost certainly have given you insights into both the problem and its remedy.

Tension can also be dissipated when a character achieves her goals too easily. If you find your narrative slackening, it's often helpful to ask whether you've created enough resistance to the character's progress. There's limited value for a reader in a story whose characters easily get what they want. Interesting stories tend to be about characters making demanding journeys and negotiating difficult terrain (actual or figurative) and this means that you have to provide the impediments that increase the tension of the story and heighten readers' investment in its outcome. This holds good not only in relation to the dominant strand of a long work of fiction but also on a smaller scale: the tension of minor episodes within your narrative can be significantly heightened by attention to this matter, as the following exercise will show.

5.
Ruby has been invited to accompany her sister, Emma, to a business dinner organised by Emma's company. When Ruby goes out to fix her make-up she overhears two of her sister's colleagues discussing how they're going to sabotage the presentation Emma is due to make after the dinner. Ruby could, of course, go straight back to the dining hall and forewarn Emma, but your task here is to make this difficult for her by placing obstacles in her way. Write the scene from the moment Ruby hears the plan to the moment she finally gets back to Emma, just as she is about to step up to the lectern to deliver her talk.

It's not particularly difficult to imagine a series of plot-related obstacles that might hinder Ruby in her attempt to alert her sister to the plot against her. Perhaps she thinks it best to call Emma, but finds that her phone has been turned off; she rushes to the dining room but finds Emma deep in conversation with her boss; she scribbles a note – 'Must speak with you' – on a scrap of paper and props it against Emma's wine-glass only to see it removed a few moments later by a member of the dining room staff. But you can also heighten the tension by broadening your focus to include aspects of character and relationship. Suppose Ruby has lived her life in her sister's shadow, failing her exams while Emma passed with flying colours, suffering long periods of unemployment and loneliness while Emma's career and marriage flourished. If, as a result, she feels resentment, might she briefly consider letting Emma deal with the problem herself? If, on the other hand, she worships her sister, protecting her interests with a blind loyalty, might there come a moment at which the urge to deliver her warning threatens to derail the event and, by extension, Emma's career?

We can see tensions of this kind at work in a gripping passage in Thomas Hardy's 1873 novel *A Pair of Blue Eyes*. The central event here is very obviously designed to grab and hold the reader's attention: Henry Knight and Elfride Swancourt are walking along a cliff-top when Knight loses his footing and finds himself dangerously poised above a sheer drop. In trying to save him Elfride puts herself in danger and has to be helped back to solid ground; but in helping her, Knight makes his own position still more precarious. Knowing that he will fall long before she can bring assistance from any other quarter, Elfride takes off her petticoats and tears them into strips which she then ties together to form the rope by means of which he hauls himself to safety.

That's tense enough, you might think, but there are other tensions built into the narrative at a deeper level. Elfride has gone to the cliff-top to track the progress of the boat that is bringing

Stephen, the man she has all but promised to marry, back into her life. But Knight's arrival on the scene is no accident: he has fallen in love with Elfride and, in Stephen's absence, Elfride has come to feel that Knight is, in every way, a more attractive proposition than her previous choice. Think what this situation adds to the narrative as, just prior to losing his footing, Knight trains his telescope on the boat and sees one of the passengers, almost certainly Stephen himself, looking back at him and Elfride through his own telescope. Now set alongside that potent image the constrained but unmistakable sexual chemistry between Elfride and Knight as he offers her his shoulder to rest the telescope on, and the frisson (probably more intense for a Victorian readership than for a modern one) created by Elfride's removal of her undergarments, and you'll appreciate the skill with which Hardy gives depth and resonance to his cliffhanger episode, strengthening its hold on the reader.

The next exercise asks you to work along similar lines, taking account of circumstance, character and relationship to give depth to a dramatic incident.

6.

The incident takes place in the office of a solicitor. In addition to the solicitor there are three characters present, the middle-aged children of the recently deceased widower whose will is to be read. As the three sit waiting the door opens and a woman, unknown to any of them, sweeps in and sits down alongside them. 'And now,' says the solicitor, 'I can begin.' He opens a dusty file, takes out the will and starts to read …

We're not asking you to write out the back-story in detail, but whatever is revealed in your narrative, both by the solicitor's reading of the will and by subsequent developments, should in some way take account of prior events, as well as the characters and interrelationship of the three children. Sketch a few key details in note form before you make a start on the episode itself, which should be written in such a way as to bring out something of the wider context represented in your notes.

When you look back over the piece you've written you'll probably be aware of the relative complexity of your text and of the process that produced it. Complexity isn't valuable for its own sake, but it's often an indicator of a serious approach to writing: in this case your deliberate engagement with matters beyond the plot events that form the primary focus of the episode should have helped you to create a richer and more arresting dynamic than the events alone allow.

You'll probably have been aware as you worked your way through this section that, while pace and tension are complementaries, operating in tandem to hold the reader's attention, pace isn't necessarily productive of tension. Consider these two examples:

> a) *Anand decided it would be better to speak with Francesca face to face. He took the short cut through the back alleys until he reached the high street and then walked briskly past the shops. At the junction with Victoria Road he turned right and kept going until he reached the cinema. From there he could see the bus station and less than five minutes later he was on the number 12 bus, heading for Francesca's office.*
>
> b) *Anand decided it would be better to speak to Francesca face to face so he took the bus to her office.*

It's easy to see what's wrong with example a): clogged with inessential detail, it moves the narrative forward at a snail's pace. Example b) gets straight to the point, but you might reasonably feel that, while significantly speeding up the narrative, it's even less interesting than a). The final exercise in this section invites you to improve on both examples.

7.

Using insights gained from your reading of this section, describe Anand's journey in a way likely to pique your reader's interest and hold it throughout. If you want to avoid the pedestrian dullness of example a) without simply overleaping the journey in the manner of example b) you'll have to work inventively. Perhaps there's a matter that needs to be resolved (have Anand and Francesca

had an argument?); maybe there's a sense of urgency (will Anand get to the office before it closes?), an impediment (is his phone about to run out of juice - and he's come out without his wallet?) or a circumstance that intensifies the sense of jeopardy (who is the handsome new employee mentioned by Francesca in glowing terms on several occasions during the past week?). Work with these suggestions and/or ideas of your own to produce an account of Anand's journey at once more dynamic and more engaging than either of the examples above.

In addressing matters of pace and tension you may find it particularly helpful to enlist the help of a trusted reader, someone who can tell you where, in their view, the energy of your writing falters. Ultimately, however, you will need to decide for yourself what works and what doesn't. The exercises in this section should have given you a steer in the right direction, helping you to see more clearly how to satisfy that large body of readers whose perfectly understandable wish is to find a book they can't put down.

– 9 –
Description

Setting the scene

Beginning a novel with a detailed scene-setting description was commonplace in nineteenth-century fiction. Take, for example, George Eliot's *Romola* (1862–3), which begins with an extensive 'Proem', describing the historical period and location (fifteenth-century Florence) in which the events of the novel will be set. A proem is a preface or preamble, and as we begin to read the novel we are alerted by Eliot's use of the term to the fact that the story itself has yet to begin.

Similarly, Mary Elizabeth Braddon's *Lady Audley's Secret*, published contemporaneously with *Romola*, begins with a lengthy description of Audley Court, an ancient country house, before offering a description of its owner, Sir Michael Audley – 'fifty-six years of age … a big man, tall and stout, with a deep sonorous voice, handsome black eyes, and a white beard'.

In today's fiction there's a much greater tendency to incorporate description – whether of period, place or character – in an evolving narrative; to drip-feed it into the action of a story, offering only, or mainly, such descriptive detail as is required for the furtherance or elucidation of the plot. This doesn't mean that we should never write a sustained passage of descriptive prose, only that we need to assess the effect of such writing in the light of widespread modern practice and reader expectation.

That said, let's begin with an exercise in straightforward description.

9 Description

1.

Describe a place associated with your childhood. This could be your own family home; however, it can be helpful to choose somewhere a little less familiar, a place you visited regularly, but experienced afresh each time you did so – perhaps the house, flat or garden of a neighbour, relative or friend. If none of these works strongly for you, use any place visited in childhood that has left a significant impression on you – for example, a seaside town, an art gallery or a wild landscape.

As you read through the piece you've written, try to imagine it as part of a short story or novel. It may be a very good piece of writing and an entirely appropriate response to the prompt you've been given; but you may nevertheless see that a passage of this kind has the potential to impede the flow of a narrative.

You may also notice a tendency towards the lyrical. It's natural that a passage of descriptive prose will have a more lyrical cast than a passage centred on action or dialogue, but it's common, particularly among developing writers, for the authentically lyrical to drift towards showiness and self-indulgence. Descriptive material often needs to be checked for this kind of excess. Is your phrasing stilted or inappropriately archaic? Is the passage too densely packed with adjectives, or loaded with similes and metaphors designed more to impress your readers than to illuminate your subject?

In addition, you may want to check that your description has provided a suitably wide range of sense impressions. The human mind tends to focus particularly strongly on the visual, and we sometimes need to remind ourselves, as writers, to broaden our focus, giving space to the other senses. Open yourself as fully as you can to the experience of being in the remembered place and your description is likely to become richer and more compelling.

Finally, consider the viewpoint from which your remembered place has been described. Have you tried to immerse yourself as fully as possible in the experience as it presented itself to you at the time, or have you provided a more detached description, from your present viewpoint? As you'll appreciate, these two perspectives differ significantly from one another in their effects. Detached descriptions tend to put the story on hold, usually in order to provide an evaluation of matters that require an adult understanding, while immersive descriptions foreground the way the centre of consciousness – in this case the child you once were – responds to the setting. Immersive descriptions have the advantage of engaging readers more fully with the story, enriching their sense of the character as well as evoking the physical space the character occupies, but you may have good reason for preferring the more detached, evaluative perspective. Either way, the important point – as in all aspects of writing – is to be aware of the choices you make, and of their effects.

It will be helpful to bear these matters in mind as you move on to the next exercise.

2.

Write the opening of a novel or short story – a passage that serves to set the scene, introduce at least one significant character and set the action going. The passage will naturally be descriptive, but you should work to ensure that your description has the energy and vividness necessary to drive the narrative forward and engage the reader. Work with a light touch, allowing descriptive detail to emerge from your writing rather than setting it down as a solid block of information. You may find it helpful to look back at the discussion of beginnings in Section 7 before you start this exercise.

This wasn't presented (as the first exercise was) as an exploration of memory, but you'll appreciate that, as suggested in Section 1 (Memory and imagination), our fictions inevitably draw on our own personal experiences. The lumpy mattress you had to lie on when you visited your grandparents' house may enter your fiction as a reason for a character's wakefulness; or a recollection of unfamiliar birdsong heard on your first trip abroad may be used to accentuate a fictional character's sense of disorientation as he wakes in a squalid hotel room in a foreign country with no passport, no money and no recollection of how he got there.

Emotion in description

Whether we're recording actual memories or writing fictions partially derived from those memories, we're likely to be aware of the importance of emotion as a component of our descriptions; indeed, an emotion is as likely to be our point of entry into a narrative as an image or an idea. It's not, in general, particularly helpful simply to name emotions – the reader will quickly tire of being told that characters are sad or happy, angry, frustrated or frightened – but we can charge our fictive descriptions with emotion by drawing on our own memories and adapting them. The next exercise invites you to do exactly that.

None of us will have experienced exactly what the parent of a First World War soldier would have gone through in the situation outlined below, but most of us will be able to call up some comparable experience. This is the emotional capital you'll need to draw on to write this scene.

3.
> It is 1917 and Frank is expecting his soldier son, George, to come home on leave from active service in France. As he watches the street from his bedroom window, he sees not his son, but the telegraph boy approaching. (A telegram at this time was very likely to bring news of a fatality or a serious injury.) Write a descriptive scene with Frank as the centre of consciousness (first person or tight third-person narrative) from just before he sees the boy to the moment at which he is handed the telegram.

If, in writing this piece, you sensibly avoided the obvious (such as, for example, 'Frank was extremely worried that the telegraph boy might be bringing bad news about George'), how did you imbue your description with a sense of anticipatory fear? Perhaps you focused on the setting (lowering clouds and rainswept streets might provide an appropriate atmosphere of foreboding) or perhaps on Frank's actions (he might pace the room, fold his hands in silent prayer or hover anxiously at the head of the stairs, leaning over the banister to hear whether the boy's footsteps pass his house or slow at the front gate). Then again, you might have tried a different approach: would it perhaps be interesting to have the boy arrive on a morning of bright spring sunlight, at a moment when Frank's spirits are lifted in expectation of his son's imminent arrival? Or might Frank be so agitated that he would look at anything but the approaching telegraph boy – a passing dog, an empty cigarette packet blowing down the street, sunlight glinting off a neighbour's window pane – to avoid confronting his fear? The possibilities are legion; the important thing is to select your details with care to ensure that your description carries emotional weight.

Putting yourself in Frank's shoes, you have probably recalled and put to use your own emotional experience of fearful anticipation, as well as your observations of this state in others. This may have manifested itself in various ways, perhaps including a sense of time expanding; an inclination to read the signs (the angle of the telegraph boy's progress down the street, for example, or the expression on his face as he draws closer to the house) in positive, as well as negative, ways; rehearsing receiving the news; anticipating the consequences of bad news on oneself and the reactions of others; willing, or praying for, the thing that seems to be happening not to happen; a dreamlike sensation or a sense of being apart from the event, as if observing it happening to someone else. It may be that forms of denial and preparation compete in your description; but however you have characterised Frank's feelings, what matters is how far you have been able to immerse yourself (and, by extension, your readers) in his worldview at this pivotal moment in his life.

In mapping out ways of demonstrating Frank's inner turmoil we've suggested a number of possible feelings you might want to convey, and it's worth saying here that, while you probably won't want to include all of these, you may want to explore the way in which feelings can be mixed, and even at times contradictory. Mixed feelings are difficult to write about because they are by definition confusing, but of course this quality is part of the emotional truth of the situation, and writing that strives towards authenticity must sometimes acknowledge and embody this confusion. If we want our characters to think and behave like real people, we may at times have to depict them as being at the mercy of their feelings, unable to make complete sense of them. It's our job, as writers, to describe human experience in such a way as to reflect the tensions and contradictions that repeatedly disrupt or complicate it. We need to accept that poise and clarity may sometimes be sacrificed in favour of descriptions that reflect the ragged, unstable shape of ambivalent or conflicting emotions.

Describing a character's surroundings

Let's now continue Frank's story, with an exercise that shifts the perspective slightly, focusing more strongly on his surroundings – on the world external to his fears and hopes. You'll be aware that when we write freely it's usually neither possible nor desirable to effect a neat separation between inner and outer worlds, but for the purposes of this exercise it may be helpful to remind yourself of the notional difference between the two.

4.
>Frank goes into the sitting room and reads the telegram. He learns that his son is alive and in England. He is in hospital and out of danger, but has sustained a life-changing injury. Write a passage that addresses these matters, while privileging description of the room.
>
>This exercise asks you to consider the question of Frank's mixed feelings (probably, in broad terms, a combination of relief that his son is now out of the war and anxiety about what his injuries may mean in terms of his future) while giving significant weight to his surroundings, exploring the way they impinge on

him at this difficult juncture. Perhaps a photograph of George sits on the mantelpiece, reminding Frank of his son's childhood; perhaps a rip in the fabric of a cushion calls to mind an occasion when George, in defiance of his parents' prohibitions, brought his friends into the room and caused the damage while larking about; or perhaps Frank wonders how the room will need to be adapted in the light of George's disability. Of course there are feelings here, and they shouldn't be excluded; but see what you can do to give a sense of Frank's experience in a description that focuses largely on the room and its contents.

You'll be aware that in directing you towards details that reinforce Frank's feelings we restricted the focus of your description, and this is deliberate. Good description is selective, and the writer's selections should be made on the basis of their relevance to the story in which they appear. Descriptions of place are important, providing a context for the characters and their actions, but the task of the fiction writer isn't to provide the kind of comprehensive inventory that might be supplied by an architectural surveyor or an estate agent. Description that functions merely as filler or decoration will have far less impact on the reader than description that serves a purpose, playing its part as an active ingredient in the scene or moment. It's worth bearing in mind in this context the general point that providing too much information in a narrative may actually close down the reader's imagination: it can be far more effective to provide a few well-chosen details – catalysts for imaginative engagement on the part of the reader – than to attempt a more exhaustive description.

If you ever get bogged down in a descriptive passage, try asking yourself this question: 'Why am I describing these details?' If your answer is simply 'Because that's what I see', you may need to re-examine the details, considering alternatives that relate more specifically to the story you want to tell. A better answer – the answer that will tell you you're on the right track – might be: 'Because that's what my character sees'. Think about this as you reflect on the previous exercise, and bear it in mind as you embark on the next.

Unfamiliar surroundings

As a writer of historical fiction, Hilary Mantel was acutely aware of the dangers of slipping into description merely or primarily as a means of instructing the reader about a narrative's historical context. Observing that 'people don't notice their everyday surroundings and daily routine' (and thereby implying that the writer might be well advised not to register these things in a fictional narrative), she suggested that one of the ways of lending plausibility to description is to show characters responding to places or circumstances with which they themselves are unfamiliar. Although writers of fiction need relevant knowledge (and Mantel researched her subjects in depth) the important question for them is not so much 'What do I know about the world my characters inhabit?' as 'What are the details that would catch the attention of my character?' The next exercise invites you to explore this question.

5.
Here are two related scenarios. Taking whichever seems more interesting to you, write a first-person or tight third-person passage largely focused on (though not necessarily restricted to) their surroundings.

(a) Tilly, a student from an economically deprived inner-city area, has won a scholarship to a prestigious private school. Unlike her old comprehensive school, this is a single-sex institution, steeped in history and housed in an imposing old building in extensive grounds. Almost without exception, its students come from privileged backgrounds.

(b) Alex, a privately educated student from a privileged background, is obliged by his father's bankruptcy to move to a new school. Unlike his old school, this school was built in the

1970s, in the middle of a high-rise housing estate of the same period; it is a co-educational comprehensive school and its students are drawn from a much wider social and economic range than he is used to.

In each case the character knows nobody at the school. Due to an administrative problem each arrives after the start of term, with instructions to report to the head teacher's office.

Describe the school from the point of view of your chosen character as s/he moves through the unfamiliar environment, from the school gates to the Head's office. What details are likely to strike your character most forcefully? Can you use those details in such a way as to suggest your character's feelings?

Whichever exercise you choose, your writing will have reflected something of the worldview of the character, with priority given to those aspects of the environment that are most striking to them in the light of their previous experience. Looking back at what you've written you'll see that the description of place is not objective – each school is what it *appears* to be to the character who has just entered it – and you'll understand from this that description can be used to inform the reader both about the place itself and about the character from whose viewpoint it is described.

Familiar surroundings

Hilary Mantel was certainly right to suggest that having a character visit an unfamiliar place can provide an ideal opportunity for description; however we may often need, in the wider interests of our narrative, to depict surroundings with which our characters are familiar. The next exercise will help you to explore how this might be done in ways at once informative, plausible and engaging.

Let's say we want to give the reader a sense of Dylan's regular place of work. For the purposes of our narrative, we've decided it's important to convey the information that his workplace is a café, that the café's furnishings and decor are outmoded and shabby, and that the menu is uninspired. Here's one possible approach:

> There was an art to unlocking the door, just as there was a work-around for so many things at Sadie's. Dylan simultaneously turned the key and pulled the handle towards him before giving the door a sharp kick. Once inside, he shut the door and turned the sign to Open. Over the usual scent of cooking oil a top note of potato peelings and boiled cabbage informed him that Sadie had not taken the bins out yesterday. That would be his first job. Still, she had swept and washed the floor – that was something, though only an expert eye would notice the difference her labours had made to a surface so scratched and worn that it looked permanently dirty. Dylan picked his way between the tables and chairs to the counter, switched on the overhead lights and hung up his coat and duffel bag in the lobby beyond.

So far we've provided a number of hints about what kind of establishment Dylan works in, and given the reader some sense of its layout. Mentioning Sadie helped to expand the narrative's scope a little, but it's fair to say that the passage above isn't entirely engaging. It will help if there's something else going on in Dylan's life – and of course there's likely to be, because otherwise we probably wouldn't be writing about him. Let's see what happens when we introduce further details of his life into the description of his workplace.

> As he went through the routine, switching on the fryers and loading the coffee machine, it occurred to Dylan, with a sharp thrill, that if Edward were ever to come in again it might be today. He tried to picture it: Edward walking in, pushing the swollen door shut behind him, brushing his hair back from his handsome face. It would be best to act nonchalant, he thought, to pretend not to recognise him until he went over to take his order. As he imagined the scene, he transformed it: now he was the owner of the café, he had changed its name to The Soup Kitchen, he had ditched the deep-fat fryers. The sticking door had been eased, the walls were brightly painted, the plastic chairs and rickety tables had been replaced by something simple but chic. He was just weighing up the merits of black and white ceramic floor tiles when the door opened.

Obviously we can't evoke every location by having a character mentally redecorating it or falling in love in it: these are simply examples of possible strategies, designed to give a stronger sense of Dylan as an individual and thereby to engage the reader's interest more fully. The exercise that follows invites you to work in a similar vein, enriching your description of the location by interweaving it with aspects of the life of the character from whose viewpoint it is described.

6.
Kevin and Erica have been married for two years. They live only just within their means, in a house on which they have spent a good deal of money, renovating it to a high standard. One evening Kevin walks into the expensively equipped kitchen as Erica is preparing dinner and tells her that he has been made redundant. Bearing in mind lessons learned from the two examples above, describe the aftermath of this bombshell announcement from Erica's point of view, giving a sense of the kitchen's appearance and of its importance to her. It may be worth considering that, while the kitchen is a familiar space, the couple's new circumstances may significantly affect the way she sees it.

In addressing this exercise you may have found that last hint particularly helpful. The idea that she could be about to lose her dream home provides a plausible reason for Erica to linger on details that might, in normal circumstances, have passed almost unnoticed. But however you've approached the task, you should now be developing a deeper sense of the importance of selection – of searching out the details that will make your descriptions seem both interesting and appropriate.

Appropriate description

What is appropriate is determined partly by the circumstances defined in your narrative. We've already touched on this matter in discussing the description of familiar and unfamiliar locations, and it might be worth expanding the discussion here.

Look carefully at the following passage, asking yourself how appropriate the description is to the circumstances suggested by it.

> *Fortunately the front door had been left unlocked and the housekeeper was, to judge by the sound, stacking the dishwasher. Anthony tiptoed through the hallway and up the stairs, well aware that he might have only a few moments before she returned from the kitchen. He slipped into the bedroom, wincing as the door creaked. He had to find the tiepin before the police arrived to search the house.*
>
> *The bedroom was straight out of a glossy magazine – the sort of bedroom you couldn't imagine anyone actually sleeping in. The bed was enormous and heart-shaped; he wondered where anyone might find sheets to fit it. And there must have been a dozen cushions on it – why? Surely they would all have to be removed every night? They certainly couldn't be comfortable, covered as they were in sequins and buttons and beads. Andrea's atrocious taste, he thought – Roberto would never choose this stuff. Everything was shades of cream and pink and gold, the velvet curtains pinched back at the sides with tasselled golden cords, like the waists of Victorian ladies. The bottom of each of the curtains was artfully arranged to trail on the floor in voluptuous swirls like the train of a film-star's award-night gown. The wallpaper was gold too, with suggestively regal symbols in relief: a portcullis, a fleur-de-lys, a lion. Andrea had clearly been given a free hand with the decor and, he supposed, a blank cheque.*

You'll doubtless have spotted the fundamental problem here. We're viewing the bedroom through Anthony's eyes, but the description in the second paragraph takes no account of the circumstances outlined in the first. Anthony's preoccupation is twofold: he needs to recover the tiepin and to avoid being caught in the act by the housekeeper. The leisurely description of the decor may tell us a lot about Andrea's taste, but it doesn't reflect what is likely to be at the forefront of Anthony's mind as he searches, perhaps with increasing desperation, for the tiepin. The focus of the description is not only inappropriate to his circumstances but also damaging to the narrative: what should have been a taut and suspenseful scene has had all the energy drained out of it by the emphasis on matters which may not be irrelevant to the story as a whole but which clearly don't belong here. The following exercise invites you to explore ways of correcting the problem.

7.
Rewrite the second paragraph of the passage above in such a way as to make it both more convincing (what might more plausibly be going through Anthony's mind at the time?) and more effective (how might the tension be heightened?) Feel free to introduce whatever new details might help you in your task – the sudden wail of a police siren from the main road, for example, or an indecipherable silence from the kitchen.

In revising the piece you may have found that you also needed to shorten it: if Anthony's situation wouldn't realistically give him time to linger on the soft furnishings, to make artful comparisons with the garments worn by film stars or Victorian ladies, or to wonder where Andrea sources her bed-linen, most of those details will have had to go. But you may also have seen the possibility or necessity of introducing details likely to be of greater significance to him: a locked dressing-table drawer, perhaps – could the tiepin have been secreted in it? – or footsteps in the hallway – is the housekeeper about to come upstairs and discover him? However you've approached the task, the expectation is that you will have created a tighter and more compelling narrative.

Describing a person's appearance

Although physical appearance may sometimes be indicative of character, we're speaking here about details that are, by definition, more superficial than the personal qualities we discussed in Section 2. This relative superficiality doesn't mean that we should never describe any aspect of a person's appearance – only that we need to take particular care to ensure that our details are judiciously selected, and carefully worked into the fabric of our narratives.

Much of what we've said about describing place is relevant here. Although the writer needs to have a good idea of a character's outward appearance (this will help to avoid continuity errors) it doesn't follow that every detail of that picture needs to be conveyed to the reader. On the contrary: a long list of physical attributes is generally of limited interest to readers, who can usually construct a portrait from a few indicative brush strokes. And by giving readers the freedom to participate imaginatively – to elaborate, in their own minds, on the restricted information they've been given – the carefully reticent writer may engage their interest more successfully than the writer who insists on providing more descriptive detail than her narrative actually requires.

The following exercise invites you to explore ways of describing a character's physical appearance in a way conducive to the flow of your narrative.

8.
Imagine that you're setting out to write a novel or short story, beginning with an encounter that introduces the two main players to one another, and to your readers. Your task is to write an opening passage derived from the following information.

Both characters are university students. Corin, hung over and late for a lecture, is hurrying across the campus with his head down because of the driving rain. As he rounds the corner of a building he collides with Denise, sending her flying and scattering her books and papers. In describing the incident and its aftermath, create opportunities to convey something of the physical appearance of one or both of these characters. You'll find it helpful to build on the insights gained from your descriptions of place in the previous exercises.

As with the descriptions of place, it will have been important to provide a sense of movement and energy, and since the focus was primarily on active presences – our two characters – the task here was perhaps a little easier. However, it's quite possible to describe characters in flat, uninteresting ways, and it's worth bearing in mind that there are strategies for avoiding this.

Let's say that you wanted to emphasise Corin's hungover state as witnessed by Denise. An inexperienced writer might come up with something like 'She noticed his bloodshot eyes, uncombed hair and crumpled shirt, and concluded that he had been partying until the small hours'. This does the job, but that trio of simple adjective–noun combinations might justifiably be seen as an indication that the writer isn't working hard enough. A version in which Corin narrows his bloodshot eyes, runs his fingers through his tangled hair and wipes the rain from his forehead with a crumpled shirt-sleeve would be stronger: the verbs would create an energy missing from the first version, while the necessarily greater complexity of the syntax would add interest and variety to the description.

The telling detail

A well-chosen detail can carry a significant amount of weight in a narrative. Consider this, hardly more than a snapshot: a man sitting on a park bench takes a crumpled cigarette from his overcoat pocket, lights it and almost immediately stubs it out again. Is the man extremely nervous? Has his doctor told him he'll be dead in a few years if he doesn't kick his smoking habit? Is the single cigarette a sign that he's too poor to buy a pack, and depends on hand-outs from passers-by? We don't know from the description alone exactly what we're being told about the character – we may have to read further into the hypothetical narrative to find out – but the sharp focus suggests that the detail has a certain importance, and a good writer will understand the need to deliver on that suggestion.

Sometimes the telling detail is one that qualifies or subverts the main thrust of a narrative, as in this example:

> *Jessica looked fabulous. She was working the room, resplendent in a green satin dress, with a bright smile and a word for everyone. When she*

9 Description

saw me she raised her champagne glass with a delighted squeal and wriggled her way through the guests.

'That's such a fantastic dress!' I said.

'Oh, it's just the first thing I grabbed from the wardrobe. It's from a charity shop – cost a fiver.'

'Well, you look terrific. And very much on top of things.'

A slight quiver of her lower lip, but she recovered immediately. 'Must circulate!' she cried, turning back to the throng. Only then did I notice the astronomical price tag still dangling from the zip of her dress.

The quivering of the lower lip and the giveaway price tag are details that speak glancingly but eloquently of the gap between the reality of Jessica's life and the impression she is working so hard – perhaps a little too hard – to convey. With this example in mind, you can move on to the next exercise.

9.

The scene is a station platform. Evelyn is there to collect her nephew, Alan, whom she has never met. Alan is the eighteen-year-old son of Evelyn's sister, who emigrated to Australia twenty years ago and has barely contacted her since; he's taking a gap year before going to university. Working with details relating both to the characters and their location, describe the meeting. Aim to include at least one revealing detail suggesting the possibility that things are not exactly as they seem. You should feel free to include dialogue, but your primary focus should be a description of the scene as experienced and interpreted by Evelyn.

The exercise privileges the idea of the telling detail as one that brings to the reader's notice a truth not otherwise obvious from the text. (Detective fiction makes extensive use of this device, but it may play a part in any kind of fiction.) However, you'll realise as you look back over this section that its central message is that all of our details should be, in some significant sense, telling details, each working as hard as possible to illuminate, relevantly and compellingly, the scenes that form the basis of our narratives.

— 10 —

Research

The nature and value of research

In Section 1 we touched briefly on an injunction familiar to many writers: *write what you know*. We suggested there that, as we explore and articulate our memories, we may find that we know more than we initially realised; also that, where memory provides less than our narrative requires, our imaginations may fill the gap. In the present section we shall be examining a further, related suggestion – that research can usefully increase the sum of what we know, rendering our narratives more vivid and, importantly, more convincing.

Research: the term has an academic ring to it, and some of the fiction writer's research may indeed be conventionally scholarly, carried out in museums and galleries, libraries and archives. But research might also involve spending a day as a volunteer in a care home; visiting a factory, a film studio or a building site; or interviewing someone who was present at a terrorist incident. For us, as writers of fiction, research is any exploratory work we carry out in the service of our writing.

The more closely a fictional narrative conforms to the contours of its author's life, the less likely it is that research will be required, and it's quite possible to write an entire novel without carrying out any research at all. But the chances are that you have already discovered, in your writing, the need to step beyond your own lived experience and a corresponding need to establish facts that are only available to you through research.

It might be supposed that, where fiction is concerned, facts are unimportant. After all, writers of fiction make things up, so why shouldn't they make it all up, inventing whatever they please?

The answers are complex and to some extent dependent on the expectations set up by each particular work of fiction (the expectations are obviously different for a work of fantasy fiction than for a gritty realist novel set in 1950s London); but the nub of the matter is that most readers want, in some important sense, to be *convinced* by what they read. A seafaring yarn set in the 1820s won't convince knowledgeable readers if the voyage from Liverpool to New York is accomplished in a week; a crime novel set in the 1920s won't convince them if the solution hinges on DNA profiling. It is, of course, possible in fiction to play subversively with reality, but this needs to be done on the basis of knowledge, not from a position of ignorance, and your reader needs to be made clearly aware of what you're up to. Francis Spufford's *Cahokia Jazz* (2023) is set in an alternative history in Cahokia, a city closely modelled on 1922 New Orleans, and although one crucial historical step has been altered, that world is otherwise evoked with scrupulous authenticity. Whatever the complexities, facts do matter, and the exercises that follow work on that assumption.

Using your sources

Sometimes our narrative requires us to research a single detail – for example, a historically appropriate brand name, the flowering period of a specific plant, or the date a particular type of car was first manufactured; at other times it may involve an extensive programme of reading. The latter process will usually start with a trawl through a wide range of material of presumed, but not yet proven, usefulness. For present purposes we've done some of the preliminary work for you, tracking down a number of contemporary accounts of the Great Fire of London in 1666, any or all of which can be used as the basis for the exercise that follows.

> *Some of our mayds sitting up late last night to get things ready against our feast to-day, Jane called us up about three in the morning, to tell us of*

a great fire they saw in the City. So I rose and slipped on my nightgowne, and went to her window, and thought it to be on the backside of Marke-lane at the farthest; but, being unused to such fires as followed, I thought it far enough off; and so went to bed again and to sleep. About seven rose again to dress myself, and there looked out at the window, and saw the fire not so much as it was and further off. So to my closett to set things to rights after yesterday's cleaning. By and by Jane comes and tells me that she hears that above 300 houses have been burned down to-night by the fire we saw, and that it is now burning down all Fish-street, by London Bridge. So I made myself ready presently, and walked to the Tower, and there got up upon one of the high places, Sir J. Robinson's little son going up with me; and there I did see the houses at that end of the bridge all on fire, and an infinite great fire on this and the other side the end of the bridge; which, among other people, did trouble me for poor little Michell and our Sarah on the bridge. So down, with my heart full of trouble, to the Lieutenant of the Tower, who tells me that it begun this morning in the King's baker's house in Pudding-lane, and that it hath burned St. Magnus's Church and most part of Fish-street already. So I down to the water-side, and there got a boat and through bridge, and there saw a lamentable fire. Poor Michell's house, as far as the Old Swan, already burned that way, and the fire running further, that in a very little time it got as far as the Steeleyard, while I was there. Everybody endeavouring to remove their goods, and flinging into the river or bringing them into lighters that lay off; poor people staying in their houses as long as till the very fire touched them, and then running into boats, or clambering from one pair of stairs by the water-side to another. And among other things, the poor pigeons, I perceive, were loth to leave their houses, but hovered about the windows and balconys till they were, some of them burned, their wings, and fell down.

  Having staid, and in an hour's time seen the fire rage every way, and nobody, to my sight, endeavouring to quench it, but to remove their goods, and leave all to the fire, and having seen it get as far as the Steele-yard, and the wind mighty high and driving it into the City; and every thing, after so long a drought, proving combustible, even the very stones of churches, and among other things the poor steeple by which pretty Mrs. – lives, and whereof my old school-fellow Elborough is parson, taken fire in the very top, and there burned till it fell down: I to White Hall (with a gentleman with me who desired to go off from the Tower, to see the fire, in my boat); to White Hall, and there up to the Kings closett in the Chappell, where people come about me, and did give them an account dismayed them all, and word was carried in to the King. So I was called for, and did tell the King and Duke of Yorke what I saw, and that unless his Majesty did command houses to be pulled down nothing could stop the fire.

(Samuel Pepys, diary entry, 2 September 1666)

The Fire having continud all this night (if I may call that night, which was as light as day for 10 miles round about after a dreadfull manner) when consp[ir]ing with a fierce Eastern Wind, in a very drie season, I went on foote to the same place, when I saw the whole South part of the Citty burning from Cheape side to the Thames, & all along Cornehill (for it likewise kindled back against the Wind, as well [as] forward) Tower-Streete, Fen-church-streete, Gracious Streete, & so along to Bainard Castle, and was now taking hold of St. Paules-Church, to which the Scaffalds contributed exceedingly.

The Conflagration was so universal, & the people so astonish'd, that from the beginning (I know not by what desponding or fate), they hardly stirr'd to quench it, so as there was nothing heard or seene but crying out & lamentation, & running about like distracted creatures, without at all attempting to save even their goods; such a strange consternation there was upon them, so as it burned both in breadth & length, The Churches, Publique Halls, Exchange, Hospitals, Monuments, & ornaments, leaping after a prodigious manner from house to house & streete to streete, at greate distance one from the other, for the heate (with a long set of faire & warme weather) had even ignited the aire, & prepared the materials to conceive the fire, which devoured after a[n] incredible manner, houses, furniture, & everything. Here we saw the Thames coverd with goods floating, all the barges & boates laden with what some had time & courage to save, as on the other, the Carts &c carrying out to the fields, which for many miles were strewed with moveables of all sorts, & Tents erecting to shelter both people & what goods they could get away. O the miserable & calamitous spectacle, such as happly the whole world had not seene the like since the foundation of it, nor to be out don, 'til the universal Conflagration of it, all the skie were of a fiery aspect, like the top of a burning Oven, & the light seene above 40 miles round about for many nights. God grant mine eyes may never behold the like, who now saw above ten thousand houses all in one flame, the noise

& crakling & thunder of the impetuous flames, the shreeking of Women & children, the hurry of people, the fall of towers, houses & churches was like an hideous storme, & the aire all about so hot & inflam'd that at the last one was not able to approch it, so as they were force'd [to] stand still, and let the flames consume on which they did for neere two whole mile[s] in length and one in bredth. The Clowds also of Smoke were dismall, & reached upon computation neere 50 miles in length.

Thus I left it this afternoone burning, a resemblance of Sodome, or the last day.

(John Evelyn, diary entry, 3 September 1666)

Then, then the city did shake indeed, and the inhabitants did tremble, and flew away in great amazement from their houses, lest the flames should devour them. Rattle, Rattle, Rattle, was the noise which the fire struck upon the ear round about, as if there had been a thousand iron chariots beating upon the stones; and if you opened your eye to the opening of the streets, where the fire was come, you might see in some places whole streets at once in flames, that issued forth, as if they had been so many great forges from the opposite windows, which folding together, were united into one great flame throughout the whole street, and then you might see the houses tumble, tumble, tumble, from one end of the street to the other with a great crash, leaving the foundations open to the view of the heavens.

Now fearfulness and terror doth surprise the citizens of London; confusion and astonishment doth fall upon them at this unheard of judgement. It would have grieved the heart of an unconcerned person to see the rueful look, the pale cheek, the tears trickling down from the eyes (where the greatness of sorrow and amazement could give leave for such a vent), the smiting of the breast, the wringing of the hand; to hear the sighs and groans, the doleful weeping speeches of the distressed citizens, when they were bringing forth their wives (some from their child bed) and their little ones (some from their sick bed) out of their houses and sending them into the country or some where into the fields with their goods. Now the hopes of London are gone, their heart is sunk …

And if Monday night was dreadful, Tuesday night was more dreadful, when far the greatest part of the city was consumed: many thousands who on Saturday had houses convenient in the city, both for themselves, and to entertain others, now have not where to lay their head; and the fields are the only receptacle which they can find for themselves and their goods;

most of the late inhabitants of London lie all night in the open air, with no other canopy over them but that of the heavens: the fire is still making towards them, and threateneth the suburbs; it was amazing to see how it had spread itself several times in compass; and, amongst other things that night, the sight of Guildhall was a fearful spectacle, which stood the whole body of it together in view, for several hours together, after the fire had taken it, without flames, (I suppose because the timber was such solid oak,) in a bright shining coal as if it had been a palace of gold, or a great building of burnished brass.

(Thomas Vincent, *God's Terrible Voice in the City*, 1667)

1. **Write a passage of fiction based on the material above. Select the details that strike you as most suited to your narrative's needs, and feel free to adapt and expand as you see fit. The material is your starting point for a piece of imaginative writing which can include invented characters and dialogue, as well as events that are not recorded in your sources. Whatever you add or change should be plausible and appropriate, but if you find that your narrative is merely replicating the source material you may want to take active steps to free up your writing. Most helpful, perhaps, would be to identify or imagine a character other than Pepys, Evelyn or Vincent, from whose point of view the events of your narrative can be shown. How might the fire be experienced by the little boy who is taken up to the Tower by Pepys? Or by one of the boatmen ferrying people to safety? Or by a wealthy homeowner forced to abandon his house and possessions and sleep, along with his wife and children, in an open field?**

   Don't be put off by unfamiliar spellings or syntax, and don't feel you can't begin until you've understood every last detail of the source texts. Once you've gathered enough material for your purposes, start writing.

   When you've finished the exercise, ask yourself how successfully you've incorporated the material provided by your sources and how far you've been able to make the narrative your own.

We're going to keep this source material in view, bringing forward ideas that may help you with future research-based writing.

Compare the passages above with this, from the introduction to a modern scholarly account of the fire:

> *The Great Fire started on 2 September 1666 in a baker's shop on Pudding Lane. Over the next four days it spread across the city of London and beyond, destroying most of the historic core of the metropolis. Thousands of houses were destroyed and tens of thousands of people were made homeless. Dozens of parish churches and livery company halls were left in ruins and St Paul's Cathedral was gutted. The disaster took place at a vital moment in England's history, in the aftermath of the Civil Wars and the Restoration.*
>
> (Jacob F. Field, *London, Londoners and the Great Fire of 1666*, 2017)

Clear, concise and factual, the passage introduces and contextualises its subject in a manner appropriate to its purpose, but you'll see at once that – obviously and understandably – it lacks the vivid immediacy of the three eyewitness accounts. Any relevant text may provide useful details, but as fiction writers we're likely to be drawn particularly to those that offer the most powerful stimulus to the imagination.

Which details in the eyewitness accounts stood out for you? Perhaps it was Pepys returning to his bed and going back to sleep while the fire took hold, or the pigeons he saw falling from the air with their wings burned; perhaps it was the terrifying soundscape – the 'noise & crakling & thunder of the impetuous flames, the shreeking of Women & children' noted by Evelyn, and the 'Rattle, Rattle, Rattle … as if there had been a thousand iron chariots beating upon the stones' of Vincent's account; or perhaps you were impressed by the disconcertingly beautiful image of the Guildhall shining like 'a palace of gold, or a great building of burnished brass'. Then again, it may be that what struck you most forcefully was the way all three writers pile up detail upon detail in long catalogues whose loose, erratic structure reflects the panic and confusion of the event itself.

Beyond the facts

As you'll appreciate, we're beginning to extend our sense of what fiction writers might be looking for when they research their subjects. Facts, as we noted earlier, are important, but our research should be something more than a quest for facts. We need to remain open to suggestions and impressions, to ideas that may have little or no basis in fact but have the power to influence our writing at a profound level. We don't need to believe in the concept of divine intervention, or even in the existence of a divinity, to understand why Vincent, like many of his contemporaries, viewed the Great Fire as a punishment visited upon the city by God; and when he suggests, as he does elsewhere in his account, that the fire was started deliberately as part of a Catholic plot, we don't need to take his improbable conspiracy theory as historical fact in order to appreciate its potential as the basis for a work of fiction.

If you'd like to explore that potential, try the following exercise:

2.
Write a first-person narrative from the viewpoint of someone who believes both that the Great Fire has been started by Catholics and that it is a punishment from God. The central subject of the narrative is an incident observed (and perhaps participated in) by your narrator at the height of the fire. Try to let his views emerge incidentally from his recounting of the incident rather than having him deliver them as blunt statements. Feel free to draw on the descriptions in the three passages above, but free also to develop and adapt them in line with the needs of your own narrative.

You may have recognised in Vincent's account a greater emotional distance than in the other two passages: where Pepys is explicit about his distress, troubled about the fate of named individuals and revealingly repetitive in his use of the word 'poor' (poor little Michell ... poor people ... poor pigeons'), Vincent introduces his description of the human suffering caused by the fire with an elaborate phrase that locates grief with an unspecified other ('It would have grieved the heart of an unconcerned person to see …'). The historian or literary critic might reasonably observe that, as part of an extended sermon, Vincent's account serves a different purpose from that served by the two diary entries; that it might have been framed after the event rather than in the heat of the moment; and that Vincent might, in actuality, have been every bit as sympathetic as Pepys. But for the fiction writer the debate may be irrelevant: that faint hint of distance may provide the key to a voice, a viewpoint, an entire novel.

We need to keep our antennae finely tuned if we want to pick up on these more delicate vibrations, these matters of something less solid than fact. Imagine someone writing a novel set in the early nineteenth century, chronicling the life of the eldest son of a family of timber merchants. She feels a need to add to her limited knowledge of what the family's work entails, so she browses the library shelves or types in a few relevant search terms, and at some stage in her researches she comes across this passage:

> *My two favourite Elm trees at the back of the hut are condemned to dye it shocks me but tis true the saveage who owns them thinks they have done their best & now he wants to make use of the benefits he can get from selling them – O was this country Egypt & was I but a caliph the owner shoud loose his ears for his arragant presumption & the first wretch that buried his axe in their roots shoud hang on their branches as a terror to the rest – I have been several mornings to bid them farewell – had I £100 to spare I would buy their reprieves – but they must dye.*
>
> (John Clare, letter to John Taylor, 7 March 1821)

Fact-focused research might home in on the figure of £100, broadly suggestive of the high value of elm timber at the time of Clare's writing (£100 in 1821 is equivalent to £9,000 in 2024), but the fiction writer might be more strongly drawn to the preceding material. Clare's grief and rage, springing from a powerful sense of relationship with the threatened trees, are the driving force behind his diatribe, and we might imagine our hypothetical writer-researcher tapping into these emotions and discovering in them an unexpected source of inspiration. Suddenly she has an additional character, a person whose violent opposition to her protagonist's day-to-day activities gives new energy to her narrative and suggests plot developments of a kind she hadn't contemplated before beginning her research.

Let's now take this out of the realms of the hypothetical, with an exercise that draws on the feelings expressed in the passage above.

3.
Write a scene in which a character, woken by a noise outside, looks out of her window one morning to see work going on in the field beyond the garden. Two men are cutting down the tree in whose branches she used to play as a child. She throws on her clothes and runs outside.

In narrating her confrontation with the men, let her feelings be embodied in her words and actions rather than being explicitly named. Don't feel constrained by the specific historical context suggested by our example above: if you prefer to set the scene in some other period, including the present, go ahead.

You'll appreciate from this example that research can be far more than an exercise in fact-finding or fact-checking; at times it may prove inspirational (as, for example, with Toni Morrison's research for *Beloved* (1987), which provided the groundwork for a visionary understanding of the novel's protagonist), and this is more likely to be the case if we approach our research-based tasks with a wide-ranging and receptive mind. Wide-ranging shouldn't, of course, be taken to imply an indiscriminate gathering up of everything that comes our way: as fiction writers we need to be able to recognise when research threatens to swamp our art, whether by distracting us from the essential business of writing or by clogging our narrative with material irrelevant to our creative purposes; but it's also worth bearing in mind that we can't always know in advance exactly what we're looking for, or what will best serve our needs. As Julie Otsuka explained in a 2010 interview, an authentic sense of the world of the story is the priority: 'I had to know how things happened, and when, and how things looked ... so that I felt I could tell the story confidently.'

The world around us

We've focused so far on research for historical narratives, but a present-day narrative may also require research. A work of crime fiction with a contemporary setting might require its author to find out – for example – the effects of a particular poison; what kind of equipment a skilled burglar might use to break into a well-protected house; or how long it takes to travel by train from one specified location to another.

All these subjects can be explored in libraries or online, but there's often added value for the writer in approaching them more closely. You'd be crazy to take the poison, and ill-advised to set up a day's work-experience with a burglar, but you might well want to speak to a medical professional or a detective as a means of gaining deeper insight into your subject than your written sources provide; and while it's easy to consult a railway timetable, there may be an argument for taking the train journey yourself rather than simply noting its duration. You'd need to weigh the expenditure of time and money against the value to your narrative of detailed knowledge, and you might reasonably come to the conclusion that the journey isn't worth it; but it's also possible that your work would be enriched by the experience. When it comes to research writers have to be realistic about what is possible and/or necessary, but if you feel that it's important to the detail and texture of your narrative that you spend a week absorbing the atmosphere of, say, an Algerian market-place or a French monastery, it may be worth following your instinct.

For the next exercise, however, we'll take a more modest approach.

4.
> Describe an incident in a workplace, understanding the term in its widest sense – a trawler or a cornfield is as much a workplace as a bakery or a classroom. Don't use your own place of work – this would largely obviate the need for research; be specific in your choice – for example, not just a shop or an office, but a greengrocer's or the office of a solicitor; and let the incident be related in some way to the work in question.
>
> Use any resources at your disposal, bearing in mind the added value of getting close to your subject: a recruitment leaflet may give you relevant information about army life, but a conversation with a serving soldier is likely to provide deeper insights.
>
> It's very easy to get carried away by research, so it will be helpful to give yourself a reasonably tight time limit for this exercise, restricting your research to a few key details – just enough to convey the sense, in your writing, that you know something of your chosen workplace and the work carried out in it. It will also be useful to decide on the nature of your incident first, to provide a focus for your research.

The time limit will serve to remind you that while research can lead us into fascinating new areas of knowledge, writers of fiction may need to exercise restraint in the interests of getting on with their primary task. There's always more to be discovered beyond the horizon, but there comes a point at which we know enough of the territory to be able to begin writing. However, this restraint needs to be balanced against the receptiveness mentioned above, and we also need to bear in mind that tightness of focus is a variable, depending on the nature and length of our narrative. With all this in view you may now want to move on to the final research-based exercise, designed to give scope for wider exploration.

Investing in research

For reasons that will become apparent as you read on, the following exercise will inevitably demand a greater investment of time on your part than any of the other exercises in this book. We'll discuss this matter in a moment, but first, here's the exercise:

5.
  The historical setting is World War Two (1939–1945) and your task is to produce a passage of fiction, perhaps (though not necessarily) a complete short story, drawing on your research into the events of the period. You'll find a wealth of resources readily available online: we'd particularly recommend the BBC's *People's War* archive and the collections of the Imperial War Museum. There are also many books dealing with the subject, from personal memoirs to broad historical accounts of the conflict.

  The field is vast, and you might find it helpful to focus strongly on the experience of one particular character on one particular day; you might also be helped by a few suggestions as to the role of that character in the action described in your narrative. Try one of the following, or search for an alternative in your source material:

  a) a combatant in one of the armed forces

  b) a nurse working in a military hospital or a bombed city

  c) a munitions worker

  d) a conscientious objector

  e) a school-age evacuee

If, after reading these directions, you feel that the exercise represents too great a time-commitment at present, don't worry. It may be that a novel or short story you're already writing demands research of similar scope but in a different field, and that you'd rather devote your time and energies to that – a perfectly satisfactory alternative. Or you may decide that it would be more convenient to come back to the exercise later, when time permits – a reasonable decision. If, however, your reason for avoiding the task is a more general resistance to research, it's worth considering the possibility that this is a good moment to take up the challenge. Research can sometimes feel like a distraction, an intrusion into the time we've set aside for our writing, but it's actually an integral part of the process.

You might also bear in mind that in taking on a project of this kind you won't simply be enhancing your understanding of the topic you're researching; you'll also be developing the skills fundamental to all research, and finding how best to use those skills in the service of your writing. If you've only recently begun to write fiction your existing store of knowledge may have carried you through up to now, but at some point you'll almost certainly find that it isn't enough. Yes, write what you know – the advice is sound as far as it goes – but be prepared to extend your knowledge as a means of advancing your writing.

– 11 –
Editing

~

The pattern followed so far in this book has tended towards firmly structured guidance, with each section designed to illuminate a particular topic, and each exercise bookended by an explanatory preamble and a passage reflecting on some of the issues you're likely to have encountered during your engagement with the exercise. The present section necessarily ranges widely over a variety of topics covered in the earlier sections; it also relaxes its guidance a little, asking you to approach each exercise without the assistance of a preliminary explanation. Each passage offered for your editorial scrutiny foregrounds a particular issue, discussed in the reflective material that follows it; however, your editing may have identified additional missteps and infelicities, or perhaps simply picked up on things you might have tackled differently, and this is as it should be. The idea is to let you decide for yourself in what ways you would improve each passage.

The process of writing can be simplistically but helpfully viewed as having two very different aspects. Much of your work will involve a significant degree of immersion in the world of your fiction and a fluid and sometimes inspirational approach to the words chosen to communicate your vision; but when you prepare to edit you need to adopt a less immersive approach, standing at a critical distance from the text, and trying to see it as if for the first time – a notoriously challenging exercise. In this section you'll be working on texts written by someone else, which should make your task easier; when editing your own work you'll probably need to keep reminding yourself to step back from the words on the page, and from much of what you know – or think you know – about them.

In each case you'll be invited to read a text and address any issues requiring editorial attention. Here's the first exercise.

1.

Pippa was furious. It seemed to her that some of her colleagues didn't understand even the basic fundamentals of the organisational structure of the business. She had thought there was a consensus of opinion in the office that Sadie would manage foreign imports while Mahada would keep the records, as had been the usual custom when Robin had run the department.

She knew it had been a mistake to let them share an office. Working in close proximity had resulted in their roles merging together and she would now have to completely disentangle them. She faced a difficult dilemma as she needed to avoid a direct confrontation, while spelling out in detail their respective areas of responsibility without adding additional stress to the existing tense atmosphere.

This could not be postponed until later, she decided. She would call a meeting for ten a.m. the following morning and sort out the whole horrible mess.

You probably realised that the central problem with the passage is the redundancy of some of its elements. Does it matter if the same thing is being said twice, or otherwise unnecessarily? Yes, it does, because unnecessary material will clog your prose, reducing its energy and effectiveness. Let's go through the passage, highlighting its redundancies.

Fundamentals means 'basic principles' – so *basic* is redundant; *structure of the business* implies organisation, so *organisational* can be deleted; a *consensus* is an agreement and the phrase *of opinion* adds nothing to the reader's understanding; what is customary is, by definition, usual, so *usual* can be deleted as well. Similarly, you'll realise that we don't need *together* with *merging*, *difficult* with *dilemma*, *direct* with *confrontation*, *in detail* with *spelling out* or, of course, *adding* with *additional*. To *postpone* means to put something off, so *until later* can be dropped, as can *a.m.* which is covered by *the following morning*.

This last example raises a complication. Looking at the passage in isolation, we might ask ourselves whether *ten* should be deleted along with *a.m.* on the grounds that the precise time doesn't matter. The self-evident truth is that it doesn't matter unless, in the wider context of the work, it does: the timing might be an important plot detail if, for example, a device had been set to explode in the office building at ten o'clock. Context must to some extent determine our approach.

A couple of further complications. What about the phrase *in close proximity*, where closeness is implied in *proximity*? On the face of it, it might seem that we could simply delete *close*, but the phrase *in close proximity to* has a contemporary currency, while *in proximity to* sounds stilted to the modern ear. This might suggest a case for retaining *close* – unless you decide to sidestep the dilemma by substituting a less problematic phrase.

Or you might wonder whether *completely* in *to completely disentangle* should be deleted as unnecessary. On the one hand, the meaning is clear enough without *completely*; on the other, the inclusion of the word heightens our sense of the radical nature of the corrective action envisaged by Pippa. For some readers the debate might be influenced by an issue unconnected with redundancy: the phrase *to completely disentangle* is a split infinitive, once a grammarian's bugbear but now widely regarded as acceptable, particularly where avoidance comes at the cost of fluency. Where you stand on this matter may determine your editorial decision.

These last two examples suggest the need for a degree of openness and flexibility in your editing. Re-reading your work with an editorial eye, you will sometimes discover details that are simply and obviously wrong – a misspelt word, for example, or the inadvertent omission of a punctuation mark – as well as many problems which are less easy to resolve. Some of the latter may create genuine dilemmas – dilemmas you need to address for yourself, working not with a set of rules but with a nuanced awareness of the needs of your text and the qualities of your own individual voice.

11 Editing

Now that you have a clearer sense of the general territory, we'll continue our editorial explorations. How would you edit this piece?

2.

    'What do you mean?' Celine asked uncomprehendingly.
    'I mean what I say,' Roman snapped. 'It's not difficult to understand. I mean: you're banned.'
    'Banned?' Celine queried.
    'Read my lips,' Roman snarled. 'You can't come here any more. Your presence is no longer required.'
    'But I don't understand!' Celine exclaimed emotionally. 'What have I done?'
    'You've only gone and broken it,' Roman insisted.
    'Broken what?' Celine enquired tremulously.
    'The unwritten law!' Roman shouted angrily. 'You've broken the unwritten law!'

We exaggerate, of course, but problems of the kind on display here are common in the work of developing writers. You probably identified the material surrounding the dialogue as the most obvious of the passage's problems: the tendency to attribute dialogue regardless of whether or not attribution is necessary; the use of unusual verbs in a distractingly strenuous attempt to avoid the simple 'said' or 'asked'; and the over-use of adverbs indicative of the way the characters' words are spoken.

Again, the matter isn't quite straightforward. We might feel that the phrases *Roman snapped* and *Roman snarled* are both stronger than *Roman said*, economically demonstrating his anger and general unpleasantness; however, we might then decide that one of these phrases was sufficient to make the point, and that the other should therefore be dropped.

Phrases such as *Celine queried* and *Roman insisted* are less obviously open to debate: whatever you may have been taught in school about the need to vary verbs relating to speech, 'said' and 'asked' should nowadays be your default, with other verbs being used only when they contribute helpfully to your text. The indiscriminate quest for variety in this matter tends to produce verbal oddities that distract the reader from what is being said in the dialogue. You might conceivably make an argument here for the retention of *Roman insisted* but *Celine queried* would be unlikely to survive a rigorous edit.

And what did you do with *Celine asked uncomprehendingly, Celine exclaimed emotionally, Roman shouted angrily* and *Celine enquired tremulously*? To say that adverbs should never be used in contexts if this kind is too sweeping a statement, but it's fair to say that none of these examples justifies its presence in the text. When, as here, a character asks what another character means, incomprehension is implicit in the question, so *uncomprehendingly* can go; similarly, Celine's emotion is evident in the dialogue and doesn't need the reinforcement provided by *emotionally*, while Roman's anger has been apparent throughout the passage, so *angrily* can be edited out. *Celine enquired tremulously* is a slightly different case since tremulousness isn't necessarily implicit elsewhere in the passage, but a stringent edit would probably remove this adverb too. If, in this particular case, you wanted to retain the idea of tremulousness, you might have tried locating it elsewhere – in, for example, a physical response: *Celine's lower lip trembled*. It's a small alteration but it strengthens the text and breaks up a pattern that has become, by this stage, wearisomely repetitive.

In editing for repetitiveness, you may have noticed that most of the recurrent attributions are unnecessary. Where a passage of dialogue involves only two speakers it is particularly easy to omit attributions or, as editor, delete them: if the dialogue is appropriately punctuated, the alternation of voices usually requires no other signposting. We shall see in a moment how this particular passage might be edited for unnecessary attributions.

Before we do so, let's highlight one further form of repetition, occurring within the dialogue itself. In editing the dialogue it may have struck you that there is something repetitive in the speech of

11 Editing

both characters, but you may also have considered the possibility that some of this is either unavoidable or actively illustrative of what is taking place between them: Celine's insistent questions reflect her incomprehension, while Roman speaks in broadly repetitive terms (*you're banned, you can't come here any more, your presence is no longer required; the unwritten law, you've broken the unwritten law*) because he isn't getting through to her. So on the one hand it might be argued that the context enforces a degree of repetition; on the other, it might be objected that repetition, however appropriate to the context, may nevertheless try the patience of the reader. This equivocation reinforces the point we made earlier – that good editing proceeds not from the wholesale application of inflexible rules, but from a nuanced assessment of what is entailed in each individual alteration.

Now let's consider an edited version of the passage, a version which takes into account the various matters we've just discussed.

> *'What do you mean?' Celine asked.*
>
> *'I mean what I say,' snapped Roman. 'It's not difficult to understand. I mean: you're banned.'*
>
> *'Banned?'*
>
> *'Yes, that's right. You can't come here any more.'*
>
> *Celine's lower lip trembled. 'But I don't understand!' she said. 'What have I done?'*
>
> *'You've only gone and broken it.'*
>
> *'Broken what?'*
>
> *Roman slammed his fist down on the tabletop. 'The unwritten law!' he shouted. 'You've broken the unwritten law!'*

This isn't the only way the passage might be edited, and you may have produced something significantly different, but you'll probably appreciate that this version is a tighter, stronger and more varied text than the original. Close comparison of the two should help you to understand more clearly the editorial process by which a passage of dialogue can be improved.

Before we leave this exercise, let's home in on two linked details illustrative of the possible complexity of the process. An interim version placed the detail of Celine's trembling lip later in the text: *Celine's lower lip trembled. 'Broken what?' she asked.* But as soon as we altered the next line we saw a problem: the structure of that line – *Roman slammed his fist down on the tabletop. 'The unwritten law!' he shouted* – resembles the pattern of its immediate predecessor too closely. A minor problem, admittedly, and it wouldn't be unreasonable to argue that the resemblance doesn't matter. But to some writers such details do matter, and we're going to suppose that you're one of those writers – that you'll understand why we chose to disrupt the pattern, creating a greater distance between *Celine's lower lip trembled* and *Roman slammed his fist down on the tabletop.* However, the change produced another problem: the clashing effect of *Read my lips* and *Celine's lower lip* on adjacent lines. How would you have dealt with this? Reverted to the original? Or addressed the problem by substituting – as we have done – another phrase for one of the clashing elements? Choosing the first option would probably speed up the editing process, and this isn't a negligible consideration; but a willingness to spend time on subtle adjustments to a text is the mark of a conscientious editor.

For the next exercise, let's move from dialogue to monologue. Consider the following passage carefully before writing an improved version.

3.
    Rosie scanned her phone and made for the door. 'Sorry,' she said, but I have to take this.' She went out into the hall, closing the door behind her. 'Eva!' I heard her say. 'You're back!'
    I moved closer to the door, listening.
    'You've been in Paris! You won a Eurostar competition and had to take the prize of a long weekend straight away... You took Matt with you? But isn't he married? And now his wife wants a divorce!... You weren't expecting her to kick him out and now he wants to move in with you, and he can't because

he'll find out about Kevin and Kevin will find out about him. How do you get into these situations, Eva? Well, I've got to go, Mo's here… No, of course I won't say anything.'

I stepped quickly away from the door and picked up a magazine.

As in the unedited version of the previous passage, the problems in this piece are exaggerated but not uncommon, and the basic problem is that Rosie's monologue is unrealistic. You can see the writer's difficulty: this passage is a first-person narrative, so the reader will only know what Mo, its narrator, knows. However, the context makes it clear that Rosie doesn't want to share the relevant information with her: Mo must glean it from the side of the conversation she is able to overhear. As it stands, however, Rosie's monologue is creaky and unconvincing, crudely echoing what (we assume) Eva is saying.

Your main task was to fix this problem, editing the text in such a way as to ensure that the narrator (and thereby the reader) is more plausibly provided with the relevant information. How did you handle this?

You probably realised that if Rosie is going to repeat any of the information Eva is giving her, there has to be a reason: perhaps it's a poor signal, perhaps there's background noise, perhaps Eva is speaking quickly, quietly or indistinctly, or perhaps Rosie is having difficulty processing the information – you might have made use of any of these possibilities. You may also have decided to have Rosie ask questions – though these would need to be questions that would be considered reasonable in the circumstances, and you'd still need to avoid having her simply repeat Eva's answer. And you may well have seen the value of implying, rather than merely echoing, Eva's presumed words by letting Mo hear Rosie's response to them. Here's one way you might have reworked the passage.

'Paris! Well, you could have let me know you were going. What kind of competition? Oh, fair enough, but you might have phoned, at least. Wait, did

you say Matt was with you? Slow down. Let me get this straight: you go to Paris for a long weekend with a married man and now you're surprised his wife wants a divorce? Promised? Well, maybe he did, but men sometimes feel the need to confess. What is it with you, Eva? Oh dear, oh dear... no, of course he can't move in with you. Does Kevin know? Well, that's a relief – make sure you keep it that way. I don't know, Eva – how do you get into these situations? Listen, I have to go – Mo's here. No, of course not. No, no, I won't say anything.'

Conveying information by subtle and indirect means makes demands on the reader as well as the writer; careful editing should ensure not only that a passage of this kind reads plausibly but also that the reader is able, without undue effort, to grasp its meaning.

Let's turn now to the next exercise. How would you edit the following passage?

4.

As Dulcie pushed back the door she was struck by the fact that the room was in near-darkness, the curtains still drawn even though, as she had good reason to know, Martin was an early riser who never failed to set his alarm for six o'clock and would normally, by this time, have been for a run, taken a shower and eaten his breakfast. She called his name, but there was no sound in the flat except the ticking of the clock on the mantelpiece and the dripping of a tap in the kitchen, and for a moment she hesitated, ambushed by a sudden fear that something might have happened to him. Perhaps he's ill, she thought, moving through to the bedroom and peering in, scanning the room in vain for any sign of his presence before returning to the living room, drawing up a chair and sitting down to consider her next move.

It's probably fair to say that the three lengthy sentences in this passage are sufficiently well fashioned to allow any moderately careful reader to understand what's going on, but it would have to be added that they are unwieldy, with more packed into each one than it can comfortably hold. It's not simply a question of length: it's possible to write sentences with a similar wordcount without having them stagger under the weight of their cargo. But length and unwieldiness are not unrelated, and you probably realised that parcelling up the information in smaller units could significantly improve the passage.

The devil, as usual, is in the detail. Here's a version that uses smaller units to convey the same information, yet still requires editorial attention.

> *Dulcie pushed back the door. The curtains were still drawn. It was too dark to see clearly. She knew Martin was an early riser. His alarm was set for six every morning. He would always go for a run first thing. Then he would return and take a shower. After that, he would eat his breakfast. She called his name. No sound but the ticking of the clock and the drip of the kitchen tap. She hesitated, afraid that something might have happened to him. She wondered if he was ill. She went through to the bedroom and peered in. He wasn't there. She returned to the living room. She drew up a chair and sat down. She wondered what she should do next.*

Even if you prefer this version you'll probably appreciate that it represents an unsubtle over-correction. Simply reversing the tendencies of the original passage produces a crude, staccato effect, suggestive of a failure to connect, elaborate or vary the text's component elements. This may seem obvious, but the point is worth making for the sake of the general truth it embodies: the aim of editing is to adjust the balance of a text through a careful weighing of contending possibilities.

With this in mind, you might like to consider the following pair of passages, asking yourself why – as you'll probably agree – neither is satisfactory. Having established what the central issue is, you'll then need to find a balanced solution. Feel free to play around with the material provided: the passages are simply prompts to help you focus on the essential matter of editorial balance, and balance will depend, variously, on omission or invention.

5.
   a) **As soon as Khalil opened his eyes he began to think about the day ahead – the meeting he had arranged with his line manager,**

the lunch he had made for himself the previous evening – cheese sandwiches with aubergine pickle – and the possibility of a non-alcoholic beer with Angela in the pub after work. He threw back the geometrically patterned duvet cover, slid his feet into his tartan slippers and padded across the cold floorboards to draw the floral curtains. It had rained in the night and looked as though it was about to rain again, though he remembered that the forecast was for a change around midday, with the weather clearing from the west. He shaved, using the expensive electric razor his mother had bought him, and examined his face in the mirror, noting the sallowness of his skin, the bags under his eyes and the strands of grey in his hair.

He stepped over the socks, underclothes and shoes scattered across the floor, went to the wardrobe and threw open the door. He took out his pinstriped suit and a white shirt and selected a co-ordinating tie and handkerchief. When he was dressed he went down to the kitchen to make breakfast – cereal followed by a fried egg on toast and a cup of Colombian coffee.

As he cleared the table after finishing his meal he glanced at the clock on the kitchen wall: 7.18. Plenty of time before he had to leave to catch the 8.07 train.

b) On waking Khalil began to think about the day ahead and all he planned to do in it. He got out of bed and went over to the window to see what the weather was like. Then he shaved, noting, as he looked in the mirror, the signs of ageing.

He went over to the wardrobe and chose his clothes for the day. Once dressed he went down to the kitchen and made breakfast.

Looking at the clock as he cleared the table after his meal, he saw that he was in good time for his train.

You probably saw at once that passage a) provides far more detail than is necessary or desirable – a matter already discussed in Section 8 in relation to narrative tension. The passage clearly needs heavy pruning to remove the many details that clutter the narrative without adding significantly to the reader's understanding.

However, you'll also appreciate that version b), in cutting out almost all detail, has left us with a series of colourless generalities that offer no purchase on the scenes described: *all he planned to do, what the weather was like, the signs of ageing, chose his clothes.*

In your quest for balance you will have found yourself charting a path between the two extremes represented by these passages. Specificity tends to enrich a text and engage the imagination of its readers, so the wholesale deletion of specific detail wouldn't have been appropriate: the exercise required you to identify (and possibly modify) the details which might most usefully be retained.

It needs to be acknowledged that what is most useful in a text may depend on its broader context: if, for example, the wider narrative included an account of Khalil's attempts to loosen restrictive family ties, his mother's expensive present might be a significant detail; if retaining his job depended on his meeting with his line manager, his choice of clothes would probably seem important. It might also have struck you that his examination of his face in the mirror provides an ideal opportunity for a description of his appearance: the details might profitably be retained, and even amplified.

Editing often involves attention to problems arising from the clumsy use of devices which are, nevertheless, an important part of the writer's skill set. We'll discuss this in more detail when you've identified the problems in the following passage and considered what might be done to remedy them. There's no need to produce your own version.

6.

The schoolroom was small, dark and cold. Miss Wright was a little person, proportioned more like a child than a grown woman. I knocked on the door and her thin, high voice bade me enter.

I opened the door and went in. I had the impression that the children welcomed my presence – an impression that would be reinforced when, in the first lesson of the afternoon, I heard each child read in turn. One told me, in a whisper, that her mother had given birth the previous night, while another, Bobby, mentioned that he had been given a piglet to raise. These confidences touched me and I began to feel my spirits rise: yes, I thought, I belong here. Indeed, I found Bobby waiting for me outside the gate when I left at the end of the day, eager to tell me more about his piglet.

As I stood uncertainly at the front of the class Miss Wright announced: 'This is Miss Fisher. She has come to help me transform you filthy urchins into something more closely resembling young ladies and gentlemen.'

I must not undermine her authority, I told myself, not by look, word nor deed. I cannot afford to lose this place. Not after the last time.

The last time. The incident that might easily have ended my career. I remember grabbing at the hand that wielded the cane, pushing the headmaster aside as the beaten child scrambled to his feet and made for the door.

I thanked Miss Wright and set to work, after she had handed me a register, a pile of reading books and a ruler.

We might begin our reflections by acknowledging that writers need the freedom to move backwards and forwards in narrative time. In *Heart of Darkness* Joseph Conrad establishes a temporal standpoint from which the main narrator, Marlow, reaches back through history to imagine the arrival in Britain, 1900 years earlier, of 'a decent young citizen in a toga' – a reluctant representative of the invading Roman army. This historical retrospect then leads Marlow to tell a tale drawn from his own past, a tale occasionally interrupted by his contemporary listeners and finally closed off with a return to the temporal standpoint with which it opened.

Chronological shifts of this kind are common in fiction, and often contribute significantly to a narrative's effect. So if we say that the problems requiring attention in the passage above have to do with its shifting chronology, we're not saying that it's a mistake to move between timeframes; only that, if you do so, you need to be in control of your effects. This passage, veering wildly from one timeframe to another, suggests a marked lack of control.

11 Editing

Let's track its haphazard progress. The room and the teacher are described before Miss Fisher opens the door and sees them; then, taking its cue from the children's apparent welcoming of her presence, the narrative moves us forward to the afternoon, and from there to the end of the school day, before returning to its initial standpoint: *As I stood uncertainly at the front of the class…* But we've barely arrived there before we're off again, as the narrator recalls an earlier incident that might have destroyed her career; and finally we return once more to our starting point, though with a minor twist that clumsily inverts the actual sequence of events whereby Miss Fisher was first provided with the means to work and then got on with the job.

If you recognised that the fundamental problem with the passage was a lack of control over the ordering of the narrative, you were probably able to identify a number of possible fixes; but the reason we're not suggesting that you produce a new version is that the fixing of some of the problems would be likely to involve a rewrite too radical and too extensive to be justified here. The whole structure needs overhauling and augmenting, and while this would be necessary if the passage were part of your own work, it probably wouldn't be a good use of your time in the present context.

You should, however, have formed an idea of what such a rewrite might entail. Let's look first at the second paragraph, in which the narrative catapults us suddenly forward from Miss Fisher's entry to the events of the afternoon. There's a strong argument for a more gradual, linear approach, in which we stay in the same temporal frame throughout, arriving at the events of the afternoon via a more extended account of the earlier part of the day.

Then again, your edit might address the problem by dispensing with the rather pedestrian opening and starting with the afternoon reading lesson. But (you might object) the events of the morning provide the springboard from which the narrative launches itself into an exploration of an earlier event – the intervention that cost Miss Fisher her previous teaching post. True, but that incident, dramatic in itself and apparently crucial in Miss Fisher's life, is misplaced here, not least because the narrative leaves a potentially rich scene undeveloped as it doubles quickly back to its temporal starting point.

Conventional linear chronology would obviously place the scene earlier, though placing it later can also be considered as a possibility, bearing in mind our earlier suggestion that writers need the freedom to disrupt chronological sequence if this serves the interests of their narrative; judiciously used, flashback to a past event can be a powerful device, in prose fiction as in film. But whether reinstated earlier or later in the hypothetical larger narrative, the past event can then be developed in ways its current positioning doesn't allow.

Let's turn now to another case, a passage which raises similar questions about the use – and abuse – of recognised techniques. How would you edit this?

7.
    'I need to talk to you,' said Max, pulling out the chair opposite Oliver's. 'About Dad.'
    'What about him?' asked Oliver, though he already knew what his brother was going to say.
    'It's time,' said Max. 'Time to get him a place in a care home.'
    'No,' said Oliver. 'It's not what he wants.'
    'I know that,' said Max. 'But it's not working, him being at home.'
    'It's not working for you, you mean.'
    Ollie's usual trick, thought Max – suggesting I'm the problem. 'It's easy for you,' he said. 'You're not here. You're never here – it all falls on me.'
    'Look,' Oliver said, feeling the old resentments setting in, 'you've got it easy. A place to live, the bills paid, and all you have to do in return is keep an eye on Dad. Is that really so hard?'

Max felt a sudden surge of anger. 'Yes,' he said. He stood up. 'Yes, it really is.'

For one tense moment Oliver thought his brother was going to punch him. 'Calm down,' he said. 'Calm down and sit down.'

Max snatched up his jacket, walked to the door and let himself out into the street, wondering why he'd ever expected Oliver to understand.

It would be unduly flattering to describe the shifting narrative viewpoint in this passage as a technique: the general effect is one of narratorial insecurity. Oliver is initially the centre of consciousness – the physical and emotional locus from which the interaction is experienced. The phrase *he already knew* recruits us to his perspective, and we might reasonably expect the remainder of the scene to be witnessed from that perspective. But a moment later we're admitted to Max's thoughts (*Ollie's usual trick, thought Max*) and invited to witness the scene from his point of view. From there, we're jerked back and forth between the two perspectives. You probably spotted the shifts (*'Look,' Oliver said, feeling the old resentments setting in*; *Max felt a sudden surge of anger*; *Oliver thought his brother was going to punch him*; *Max ...let himself out into the street, wondering why he'd ever expected Oliver to understand*) and you may have experienced them as a problem, evidence of a lack of authorial control. Editing to correct this problem, common among developing writers, might seem straightforward: you decide whose viewpoint you're going to adopt and you stay with it.

That's certainly what we'd recommend in the case of this passage. But it may strike you that, as with many editorial decisions, something originally present in the text would be lost in the process: if you edit the passage to reflect the viewpoint of only one of the two characters you close down access to the other character's feelings. So your editing may need to compensate in some measure for the loss, and this can be done by incorporating evidence of those feelings – evidence that might be available to the central character. Taking Oliver as your centre of consciousness you might, for example, have him see Max redden with anger or clench his fist; if you take Max as your centre you might have him see Oliver flinch from the anticipated blow.

Such additions will complicate the editing of the passage, and we need to consider a further complication: 'Choose a viewpoint and stay with it' may be good advice for most writers most of the time, but it can't be regarded as an inflexible rule. As we saw in Section 5, Virginia Woolf achieves some of her most notable effects through a fluid movement between different viewpoints, and only the most insensitive and unintelligent editing would seek to 'correct' this tendency in her work. In editing your own work you'll normally have a reasonably clear understanding of what you set out to do, and you may have begun with valid reasons for moving back and forth between third-person perspectives; you may even have the skill necessary to carry off the tricky manoeuvres involved. If, however, the shifts of viewpoint seem, on reflection, to be random, uncontrolled or clumsily executed, they need to be edited out.

The passage in exercise 7, wrenching the reader distractingly to and fro between two tight third-person viewpoints, is in obvious need of editorial correction. Often, however, the movement from one viewpoint to another is less obvious, as in the following passage. Read it through, with an eye for the moments at which the viewpoint established in the opening paragraph is disrupted.

8.
   Something wasn't quite right. Caroline had felt it the moment she arrived – a distance, an abstractedness as Adam lifted the stole from her shoulders. Now, sitting opposite him at the table, scanning his face for clues, she was struggling to suppress her anxiety.

   She picked up her glass. 'A toast,' she said.
   'What are we drinking to?'
   'Us, of course.' She tossed back her wavy golden hair and clinked her glass against his.

11 Editing

As he put down his glass she noticed a slight tremor in his hand. 'We need to talk,' he said.

It occurred to her that he might be ill. 'That sounds ominous,' she said. She leaned towards him, her diamond ear-studs flashing in the candlelight.

He drew a deep breath. 'Listen,' he said. 'I'm afraid I shall have to call off the engagement. I can't marry you.'

The room seemed to be swaying. She placed both hands on the table and stared at the ring on her finger. Her hands seemed small, vulnerable and foolish. She suddenly felt very cold.

She opened her brightly painted lips, but no words came.

You may have found it a little more difficult to see what's wrong here. The problem isn't an oscillation between the viewpoints of the two characters – we're not privy to Adam's thoughts – but an occasional slippage from Caroline's perspective to a wider viewpoint of the kind usually referred to as omniscient. It's easily done: a writer decides that the intimacy of a first- or tight third-person narrative best serves her purpose but, in imagining a scene, sees things that the central character either couldn't see or wouldn't be likely to notice. The imagining of those elements isn't a problem, and may even be helpful to the writer; but if they find their way into the text, they create fault lines disruptive to the reader's experience of the work.

Let's highlight the points at which the slippage occurs in the passage above. You probably spotted the phrases *her diamond ear-studs flashing in the candlelight* and *she opened her brightly painted lips* which provide details we wouldn't expect Caroline to be able to see, or – in her preoccupied state – to notice even if they were visible to her. But you may already have been subtly destabilised at an earlier point in your reading by *tossed back her wavy golden hair*, where the two adjectives locate us at a slight but troublesome distance from Caroline's viewpoint.

Alerted by these examples, you may have wondered about this sentence: *She placed both hands on the table and stared at the ring on her finger*. But this is a different case – not simply because what is described is something she would easily be able to see but, more compellingly, because the ring on her finger is precisely the detail someone in her position might focus on: an emblem of the promise that Adam has just broken.

Editing often involves finding workarounds, and it would, of course be possible to have Caroline catching the flash of her diamond ear-studs in Adam's wineglass or seeing her face reflected in a mirror behind him; this would address the matter of what she could actually see, but would probably leave unresolved the equally important matter of what she would be likely, in the circumstances, to notice. And it might be worth considering in this connection the general truth that over-ingenious solutions to textual problems can easily become another form of distraction for the reader. In the passage above, straightforward deletions would be the safest bet.

For the final exercise in this section we're providing you with a brief short story, complete but in need of extensive editing. Your task is to produce an edited version, conforming broadly to the text provided, but incorporating whatever changes you think will help to improve it; these may include deletions and/or additions. This may take rather longer than most of the exercises in this book, but you should bear in mind that the realistic aim isn't to produce a first-rate short story but, more modestly, to identify problems and to see what can be done, within a reasonable time-frame, to fix them. Even if the result doesn't entirely satisfy you, it's likely to be a considerable improvement on the original text.

For ease of reference we have divided the story into numbered segments.

9.

1] When they called to say there was a bed available in the drug and alcohol addiction rehabilitation unit the relief I felt was so great I almost cried. Finally we were going to get the help Mum needed – the help I needed. The help we had both needed for months.

It was a job and a half to get her out of the house, and throughout the drive I was preparing myself for her to refuse to get out of the car when we finally arrived, but in the event she didn't.

It was mercifully easy to find a parking space in front of the Larkfield Drug and Alcohol Addiction Rehabilitation Residential Unit. I am not very good at parking and I often get out to find I have parked the car 'at a jaunty angle' as my ex-husband once put it – a humorous but typically disparaging remark of the kind that eventually led to the break-up of our marriage – but on this occasion I parked the Mini Cooper beautifully, a paragon of scarlet symmetry between the white lines. Mum stepped out of the car lightly but with an audible sigh, and gathered herself while I retrieved her bag from the boot. I couldn't tell whether the sigh was one of resignation or impatience to get going: Mum's sighs were frequent and hard to read.

2] The unit was a large modern building and we entered a glass-walled reception area that seemed to belong in an artist's impression of The NHS of the Future. However the future reassuringly involved a present-day coffee shop along one side selling cakes and cookies. The customers included a mother and three badly-behaved children, a young man in scruffy jeans and trainers, a girl with a nose ring and various others, most notably an elderly gentleman, elegantly dressed in a high-collared white shirt and a charcoal-grey suit. It was impossible to tell what relationship these people bore to the environment in which they found themselves. Were they visitors? Potential residents? The recently cured awaiting a lift? There was a giant fish tank against the far wall, with a healthy population of Guppy and Platy, and tiny Neon Tetras flashing red and blue.

3] We presented ourselves at the reception desk next to the entrance and gave our names to the woman seated behind a desk that looked like a cut-price version of the bridge of the Starship Enterprise. She smiled up at us and, looking from one to the other, said: 'And who is...?' and then I realised she didn't know which of us was the one being admitted. I could see her wondering: which is the drinker? Was it the immaculately made-up, neatly coiffured lady in the Ralph Lauren beige linen suit, Hermès scarf, and kitten heels which matched her Mulberry bag? Or the wild-haired woman in the crumpled sweatshirt, grubby jeans and (but only I knew this) yesterday's socks and pants? The first was Mum, the second me. I wondered if I actually smelt as I hadn't been able to turn my back on Mum – let alone have a bath – for at least 24, no, could it be 48 hours? I made a mental note to sniff my underarms surreptitiously at the next available opportunity. Then I thought: why bother? I wouldn't be able to take a shower till I got home anyway.

'This is my mother,' I said, wanting to put an end to the receptionist's confusion.

'Gosh, I took you for sisters,' said the receptionist, smiling at Mum. Mum smiled back.

'People often say that,' I said. 'Flattering for her, not so flattering for me.'

'If you'll just take a seat over there,' said the receptionist, 'I'll let them know you've arrived.' She picked up the phone and pressed the keypad.

4] When the doctor – I supposed he was a doctor – was finally available, we went through to his office. Unfortunately Mum was beginning to become uncooperative and after the doctor had been talking for a while she became enraged, arguing with the poor man, calling him names and telling him she wasn't going to stay in the unit. But he told her she would be well looked after, that it was for her own good and that if she would agree to stay and follow the rules of the institution she would eventually emerge with an improved outlook on life. Mum didn't want to accept this at first, but after a while he won her round, and it was agreed that she would stay for a fortnight.

We were sent back to reception to sign the forms. Then the receptionist gave us two magnetic key cards, like you get in hotels. One for me to get out into the world again, she said, and one for Mum to be able to move around the unit. Mum seemed somewhat reassured by this.

5] I had to use my card three times before we arrived at the residential sector, where we were greeted by Ellen, an upbeat

Staff Nurse who took us to the main recreation area. Like the reception area it was modern and proud of it – extensive use of calm colours, an impression of light and space. A glass wall to the outside; a large well-planted courtyard garden with wooden seats and a giant chess set laid out in its centre. There seemed to be a lot of friendly staff; most of the residents were grouped around a giant TV screen, watching or asleep.

'I won't be able to stand that,' said Mum.

'There's a quiet room as well,' said Ellen.

'It's much too hot in here. Can you turn the heating down?'

'Did you have a good journey?' Ellen asked, thinking it best to change the subject. Mum was sulking, and didn't answer.

Ellen took us down one of the corridors off the main area and Mum practised using her key card on her bedroom. The room was much better than I'd expected. Light, with a large window – not a great view, mostly car park, but another little courtyard garden in front with benches and raised flower beds. It had its own en suite with a shower. The bedroom could have been out of Ikea: bright, simple, practical, clean lines. The bed was made up with a pretty indigo cotton duvet cover embroidered with daisies. It didn't feel like a hospital or any kind of institution at all. I flopped down on the armchair. 'Lovely,' I said.

6] Mum was looking a bit lost. I jumped up again. 'Let's unpack your stuff.' I put her blue silk pyjamas on the bed.

Ellen looked at her watch and let out a yelp. 'I've got to go – sorry.'

'Will you be long?' Mum asked.

'Two weeks. First holiday in years – south of France – I asked my mum if she wanted to come, knowing she'd say no and she said yes. She'll be at the door with her coat on already if I know her. You two probably want to say goodbye anyway. She put her hand on Mum's shoulder. 'You'll be fine, Elizabeth. Just go with the flow.'

As soon as she was gone Mum wanted me to set off because of the rain and the traffic. I didn't argue. I gave her a hug which she held on to, squeezing me really tight. A good sign.

'I'll miss you,' she said, still not letting go.

'I'll miss you,' I said. 'But we'll have visits, phone calls, letters if you like.'

She stepped back. 'You'd better have a wee before you go,' she said. 'It's a long journey.'

I didn't want a wee, but went into the bathroom anyway. Line of least resistance.

7] When I came back she wasn't there. But now I didn't have to worry when she was out of my sight. Not my responsibility. I felt a new wave of relief. I was really going to get my life back, for a bit anyway. She'd probably gone to negotiate the central heating being turned down for the whole hospital. I picked up my bag, took a look around the room, and went to leave.

But I couldn't open the door. I searched through my bag for the key card. I peered through the glass but couldn't see anyone. I sat down by the window, deciding just to wait for Mum rather than bang on the door and raise a fuss. The rain had stopped and the sun was coming out.

After a while I saw a familiar figure moving across the car park. My brain did a somersault and I thought to check my car keys were in my bag. They weren't. Neither was my set of documents as next of kin. I got up to raise the alarm, but something made me hesitate. I watched as the car disappeared.

I turned at the sound of the door being opened. A young woman put her head round the door and said, 'I've just come to check everything's OK.'

'Actually I'm not…' I started.

She came further into the room. 'Is something the matter?' she asked.

'No,' I said. 'It's all fine, thanks.'

She smiled and ducked out; the door closed behind her.

I considered the bed with its indigo duvet scattered with daisies. It would be such bliss to sleep, to have to do nothing, to be looked after. I looked at the blue silk pyjamas lying on the bed and started to undress.

I had wanted a break in any case, and thanks to Mum's trickery I had got my wish.

11 Editing

In editing, we're often looking in the first instance for typographical errors – simple slips in which, for example, an essential punctuation mark is accidentally omitted or two adjacent letters in a word are transposed. The passage you've been dealing with is clean in that respect but has been artificially loaded with problems of a more complex kind, often requiring careful thought and, unlike typographical errors, offering scope for a wide variety of possible remedies.

Let's begin at the beginning. We discussed in Section 7 the importance of a strong opening, and you probably noticed a slackness in the first paragraph of this story. Perhaps this began with a vague feeling, as reader, that the opening wasn't quite working; as you moved into editing mode you will have assessed the problem and experimented with possible solutions.

We've already established that a significant proportion of the editing process is the cutting of redundant material, and this opening clearly needs pruning. You might have homed in on *the relief I felt*, where *I felt* can be dispensed with because the feeling is obviously located with the narrator, or on the two following sentences, which clearly involve repetition, though there's scope for debate about what should be cut. You might have considered the simple deletion of *The help we had both needed for months*, then wondered whether the information about the length of the wait should be retained, before realising that *Finally* in the previous sentence tells the reader enough. You might also have seen that the phrase *in the drug and alcohol addiction rehabilitation unit* is clumsy, and particularly unfortunate in what should ideally be an arresting opening sentence. Certainly it provides information, but looking ahead to the third paragraph you'll see that the information is also provided there: *a parking space in front of the Larkfield Drug and Alcohol Addiction Rehabilitation Residential Unit*. Let's just say at this stage that we certainly don't need both phrases; we shall return in a moment to the question of whether we need either.

Before we leave the first paragraph, we might usefully consider *almost* in *almost cried*. It's a word we'll often do well to query. It's true that *the relief was so great I burst into tears* says something more than the original; but isn't there an advantage in intensifying the sense of relief? If you don't think so, that's fine, and *almost* can stand; but the general question is worth raising whenever a character 'almost' does something.

The second paragraph may produce a related sense of incompleteness, leading us towards an outcome that, *in the event*, doesn't materialise. If the event doesn't take place, does it need to be mentioned? If you feel a resistance to deleting the paragraph entirely, this may be because it contains the useful information that the narrator's mother is reluctant to enter the unit, but doesn't *It was a job and a half to get her out of the house* do enough to suggest her reluctance?

Moving on to the third paragraph, we might ask ourselves whether, as readers, we need to have the characters' arrival at the unit described in such detail. How important is it that the narrator isn't very good at parking? Or that on this occasion she parks well? Her failed marriage might be an important factor in a different narrative, but is it relevant to this particular story? Can we be spared the make of the vehicle, and the distracting phrasing of *I parked the Mini Cooper beautifully, a paragon of scarlet symmetry?* – not only over-elaborate but also syntactically suspect. These are all questions that need to be asked. How, as editor, you answer them is a matter of personal judgement, but it's unlikely that you'll have left this paragraph unaltered.

If you think the opening is largely unsatisfactory, you may have considered a radical rewrite. What about the following as a substitute for the whole of segment 1?

> *When they called to say there was a bed available in the rehabilitation unit the relief was so great I burst into tears. Finally we were going to get the help Mum needed – the help I needed.*

> *It was a job and a half to get her out of the house, but mercifully easy to find a parking space on our arrival. Mum stepped out of the car lightly but with an audible sigh, and gathered herself while I retrieved her bag from the boot. I couldn't tell whether the sigh was one of resignation or impatience to get going: Mum's sighs were frequent and hard to read.*

You'll realise that very little information of importance to the narrative has been lost from this streamlined version; you may also realise that the small amount that has been lost is either already implicit in other details, or can be supplied elsewhere. And the latter possibility carries with it the important suggestion that good editing isn't purely reactive but, to a greater or lesser extent, a continuation of the creative process.

Here's an example. You'll realise that, in cutting the first four words of the cumbersome *drug and alcohol addiction rehabilitation unit* in the first paragraph and deleting the phrase entirely from the second, we've removed a piece of information that might usefully have remained. Would it matter to the reader what kind of rehabilitation is needed? If we think it might, we could address the problem through a significant addition to the second paragraph:

> *Mum stepped out of the car lightly but with an audible sigh, and gathered herself while I retrieved her bag from the boot. As I lifted it over the sill I heard the clink of glass on glass. I unzipped the bag and looked inside.*
>
> *'Mum', I said, 'you promised.' I pulled out two bottles of cheap sherry and returned them to the boot. 'How could you have imagined you'd get away with that?'*
>
> *Mum shrugged. 'It was worth a try,' she said. 'I thought I might need them. Just while I settle in.'*
>
> *I slammed the boot shut and shouldered the bag. 'Let's go,' I said.*

There's no longer any doubt about the kind of rehabilitation the mother needs, and the new material adds colour and texture to a scene that was previously a little bland. If you think this new version delivers more than the deleted discussion of the mother's sigh, you may be willing to let the sigh go; if you want to keep it, you might decide to incorporate it elsewhere. That's up to you, but the essential takeaway here is that a good editor will remain open to revisions which are not narrowly corrective, but involve further creative thought and, quite possibly, a radical departure from the existing text.

And if you were worried that you might, in removing redundancies, whittle down the wordcount to a point at which there simply wasn't enough of a story left, this example holds the answer: editing may be in large part a matter of cutting inert or repetitive prose, but the cuts can be compensated for, and the wordcount built up again, hopefully to greater effect. There's another passage that may have struck you as an obvious candidate for expansion – the passage of reported speech and action in the first paragraph of segment 4. As it stands, it represents a missed opportunity, merely alluding to matters – the mother's rage, her invective, her threat to walk out, the doctor's attempts to pacify her – that could have been amplified in a powerfully dramatic scene, with a sense of immediacy provided by dialogue and with valuable tension provided by the strong possibility that she will carry out her threat. Suppose she actually leaves the room and has to be escorted back; suppose her argument with the doctor segues into an embittered criticism of her daughter's well-meaning interventions; suppose another member of staff looks in to check on the situation… Fill in the details as you like, but you'll understand the general point: that additions of this kind may amply compensate for any losses caused by rigorous pruning.

We're not going to take you step by step through the story or interrogate, on your behalf, every detail that might have benefited from your editorial attention. You'll already have a sense of the way an awkward phrase might be refined, and can probably improve (in segment 2) on both *a glass-walled reception area that seemed to belong in an artist's impression of The NHS of the Future* and *It was impossible to tell what relationship these people bore to the environment in which they found themselves.* You'll also be attuned to the recurrent redundancies in segment 3, noticing that making a point in two different ways tends not to reinforce it, and may actively weaken its impact. And you doubtless spotted the slippage from the narrator's viewpoint to Ellen's in segment 5 (*'Did you have a good journey?' Ellen asked, thinking it best to change the subject*) and probably require no clues from us as to how the problem might be addressed. It might, however, be worth looking more closely at segment 7, the story's conclusion.

We've spent some time seeking out problems in a text that has been deliberately packed with them, and this has inevitably given our analysis a strongly negative slant; but in the interests of balance, we should make it clear that a good editor is also sensitive to those aspects of a text that work well and therefore require no alteration. In editing your own writing you should take time to celebrate your successes – a well-chosen word, a finely balanced sentence, a telling image, a neat juxtaposition of ideas.

In this particular case we might notice how well, in broad structural terms, segment 7 follows and rounds off the narrative. From the start we have been aware of the mother's reluctance to follow the path her daughter has mapped out for her, and it's appropriate that her final act should be one of outright defiance. But the structure is more complex than that observation might imply: the story's opening paragraph establishes a dual focus with the phrase *the help Mum needed – the help I needed*, and much of the strength of the conclusion derives from the way that focus is maintained, with the mother's escape to freedom in the outer world matched by her daughter's escape from responsibility in the sanctuary provided by the unit.

Even so, you might have seen that some of the details of the conclusion require editorial attention. There's a strong argument for deleting *I felt a new wave of relief*, where the nervous acknowledgement (in *new*) that this is the second time in this very short story that the narrator has been flooded with relief suggests that the writer was as uncomfortable with the repetition as the reader is likely to be; and you might also have considered deleting the sentence that follows it, which is arguably unnecessary. If you wavered over this second deletion, the repetition of *back*, so soon after its appearance in the first sentence of the paragraph, might have tipped the scales.

The phrase *After a while*, at the beginning of the segment's third paragraph, usefully performs the function of moving us forward in time, but so unimaginatively that you may have considered a more interesting alternative. Perhaps you resisted *a familiar figure* in the same sentence – an unnecessarily oblique way of referring to the person the narrator must already know (and the reader will already guess) is her mother; or were underwhelmed by the inert phrase *moving across*. And you may have been troubled by the distractingly bizarre image of a somersaulting brain in the next sentence, or by the way the phrase *I thought to check* unhelpfully defuses the shock of the moment. Here, by way of example, is a version you may consider stronger:

> *I was watching the antics of two sparrows squabbling over a crust of bread when I noticed Mum dodging furtively between the vehicles in the car park. I felt my heartbeat quicken. My car keys – were they in my bag? They weren't.*

But the most obvious problem with the passage is its final sentence, an egregious example of a tendency, common in the work of developing writers, to add an explanatory note to a story that has already delivered its punch. If, in editing the conclusion, you simply struck out the final sentence, you made a wise decision.

You'll appreciate that our editorial analysis of the story has been indicative, pointing up a number of important details and issues but not aiming at comprehensiveness, let alone perfection. And this brings us to a related but more general observation: no matter how long you spend editing your work, you'll never arrive at a perfect text. But of course we're not seeking to perfect our work; only to improve it, step by step, until we feel the satisfaction of a job well done.

— 12 —
Wordplay

Introduction

Many writers will understand their craft as a form of wordplay. This doesn't mean that their work lacks seriousness, simply that it involves an approach to language that is in some sense playful. Any writer who has jotted down a phrase that adequately conveys her essential meaning, and then spent twenty minutes juggling with permutations that convey it with greater exactitude or a more pleasing cadence, will recognise the playfulness which, however serious the intention and end result, naturally informs the process of writing. It might even be argued that a willingness to spend time playing with words is the necessary basis of a serious approach to writing.

The prompts that follow give you licence to play with language. While they are unlikely to result directly in fine writing, they will encourage you to exercise the kind of verbal and conceptual ingenuity that may, in time, lead to fine writing. And many of them have the practical advantage that you can dip into them whenever you have a few moments to spare. Approach them lightly, not investing too much in them, but understanding that any or all of them may play a part in the development of your writing skills.

You'll find these prompts work well as warm-up exercises. Writers often have trouble settling down to write: stepping away from the demands and preoccupations of our everyday lives and into the world of words can be difficult, and many planned writing sessions are abandoned because the writer can't access the required state of mind. Starting your session with a warm-up exercise can help the transition from the world of activity to the world of imagination by sharpening your focus on words and ideas. You can think of warm-up exercises as a means of travelling to work – to your writing place.

Relatedly, and equally importantly, the prompts can help you when, having already started to write, you run into difficulties. It's very easy to abandon your writing when you hit a sticky patch, and often hard to pick it up again, but you can release yourself from the immediate problem by turning your attention to one or more of these exercises. Taking a diversion without actually leaving the writing zone can often improve your chances of resolving the problem when you eventually return to it.

These needn't be protracted diversions: the exercises are of varying length, but could in many cases be completed in five minutes. And you can approach them lightly, simply picking out whatever appeals to you, in any order, without any sense of obligation to complete a task once it has served its purpose.

The pleasure of words

When we write in serious mode we're usually thinking carefully about the meaning of the words we use, but there are pleasures that exist alongside, if not quite independently of, the writer's creation (or the reader's perception) of meaning. Sometimes we'll be pleasurably struck by an unfamiliar word – unfamiliar perhaps because it's archaic and/or rarely used; or perhaps because it belongs to the dialect of a particular locality. These categories can provide us with words we may never use in our writing (as writers we need to avoid using or misusing words we haven't, in the fullest sense, assimilated) but this needn't prevent us from relishing, largely for their own sake, words such as *yaffle*, *throstle*, *pettichaps* and *puddock* – all of which are archaic or dialect terms for birds now better known by other names. In the context of these exercises you can simply enjoy the rich variety of the English language without worrying about how, or whether, the words might figure elsewhere in your writing.

We might also think here of nursery rhymes and popular songs, which are not in themselves meaningless, but which young children often delight in as much for their sound as for any meaning they can glean from them. In *A Portrait of the Artist as a Young Man* James Joyce recreates a child's emulative response to a song; in the child's mouth the lines *O, the wild rose blossoms/ On the little green place* are jumbled, contracted and mispronounced to produce *O, the green wothe botheth*. And here's Joyce in *Finnegans Wake*, indulging in wordplay which, while much more sophisticated, carries with it something of the child's unfettered delight in the sound of words:

> The great fall of the offwall entailed at such short notice the pftjschute of Finnegan, erse solid man, that the humptyhillhead of humself promptly sends an unquiring one well to the west in quest of his tumptytumtoes...

What Joyce is doing here might look like automatic writing – the writer setting down whatever comes into his head – but in fact *Finnegans Wake* is a complex and densely woven text, suggesting its author's acute consciousness of his effects: its rhymes, its fluid rhythms, its conflations and coinages, puns and allusions proceed from control, not abandonment.

We're not going to ask you to compete with Joyce's dense and ingenious prose but, for your first piece of wordplay, to relax into something approaching automatic writing.

Letting go

Leaving aside those forms of automatic writing which purport to convey messages from the spirit world, let's turn briefly to surrealism, an artistic movement best known for its contribution to the visual arts but also influential on the writing of the 1920s and 1930s. In his *Manifesto* of 1924, the surrealist André Breton defined surrealism as 'thought's dictation in the absence of all control exercised by reason'. We don't need to pick this definition apart to see that it's too sweeping to work as a strategy for writing; however, a judicious relaxation of rational control provides the basis for a limbering-up exercise widely used by writers as a stimulus to creativity. The instructions are simple.

1.

Write down whatever comes to mind. Don't spend time finding fine phrases or worrying about meaning, and don't self-censor unless you feel you must. Continue for five minutes, or until you've filled a page.

Not all writers find this exercise helpful, but many enjoy the sense of liberation it offers and regard it as valuable preparation for the real writing of the day. Use it as and when needed, but with the caveat that it's unwise to make a compulsive ritual of it. You'll often find yourself ready to write without this preliminary play, and while you may occasionally salvage a phrase, an image or an idea for later use, writing produced in this way will seldom have much intrinsic value.

As you engaged with this exercise you probably realised that the very act of providing a verbal structure for the thoughts and images that passed through your mind involved a degree of rational control, and you'll observe something similar with the next exercise, a version of the technique of collage, also practised by some surrealists, both in visual and verbal form. You can see it in this excerpt from a piece assembled by the British surrealist writer Roger Roughton, 'from passages in the Evening Standard of June 6, 1936':

> Over two thousand people had taken tickets for this season's murder. Indian incense perfumed the room where people sat at ten round tables decorated with mauve and yellow irises, and were offered the choice of a succession of appetising meals and boiling bathwater up to 2 a.m.

Bear this example in mind as you address the next exercise. Although presented without any assumption that you'll be working electronically, it's essentially a cut-and-paste job, particularly well suited to that medium; adapt as seems best to you.

2.
> Take at least one short text and underline or highlight any striking phrases. (Taking two or three texts will give more interesting results, particularly if they are very different in nature – for example, a newspaper report of a robbery, a poem and an article in a magazine for railway enthusiasts.) Then reassemble your chosen phrases as Roughton has done in the example above, feeling free to supply conjunctions, prepositions and any other material necessary to maintain a fluent narrative.

You'll have been aware as you addressed this exercise that, in maintaining fluency, you've been making some kind of sense; however, it's likely that your shuffling of images and ideas has produced a number of strange and arresting juxtapositions. As with the previous exercise, you're unlikely to be able to salvage much material that will be of use to you in your more serious writing, but you may have found value (or simply taken pleasure) in the playing of the game.

The game might have been in certain respects liberating: you were freed from the need to invent by the fact that the basic material had been given to you; but you probably realised that, by the same token, you were working under a degree of constraint. We're now going to move on to examine forms of wordplay collectively characterised as 'constrained writing'.

Constrained writing

You may have come across the lipogram, a form of constrained writing involving the deliberate exclusion of one or more specified letters of the alphabet. If we take the opening line of Jane Austen's *Pride and Prejudice* –

> It is a truth universally acknowledged, that a single man in possession of a good fortune must be in want of a wife –

and exclude the letter 'l', we might rewrite it like this:

> It is a truth known to everyone that an unmarried man in possession of a good fortune must be in want of a wife.

It becomes more difficult when you exclude a vowel. Here's an example without 'a':

Everyone recognises this truth: single men with good fortunes need wives.

Excluding the letter 'e' may require even greater ingenuity:

All of us will admit that a rich man who is not a husband must long for that status.

As you'll appreciate from the examples above, lipograms are likely to produce awkward prose, but they provide an entertaining way of exercising your writing muscles and exploring the outer reaches of your vocabulary as you try, under constraint, to remain as faithful as possible to the meaning of the original. You can of course work with any piece of writing, using a passage of prose taken at random from any novel, short story, blog or news report; but here are a few sentences to get you started.

3.
Rewrite one or more of the following, excluding one vowel – you decide which.

   a) **However little known the feelings or views of such a man may be on his first entering a neighbourhood, this truth is so well fixed in the minds of the surrounding families, that he is considered as the rightful property of some one or other of their daughters.**

   b) **Nothing could have been further from that juvenile vision than the ugly hodge-podge of a building which was to serve as my introduction to the practicalities of church restoration.**

   c) **Police evacuated the area and carried out a controlled explosion, though it has since become apparent that the vehicle posed no threat to the public.**

   d) **Gradually life began to stir, though specimens of humanity were few and far between, and many of them seemed, like myself, to have nowhere to go and nothing to do.**

In the light of the difficulties you faced in making these sentences read convincingly, you may be surprised to learn that entire novels have been written under such constraints, most notably by the French writer Georges Perec, whose novel *La Disparition*, written without use of the letter 'e', was published in 1969. We're not going to suggest that you write at great length, but here's an exercise that will allow you to extend the practice.

4.
Write a short narrative of your own, operating under a similar constraint; again, you can decide which vowel to exclude.

It may have struck you as you wrote that, although extended, this was rather easier than the previous exercise, which was actually asking you to write under a double constraint – the exclusion of the vowel and the necessity of conveying the meaning of the given text; when you control the text you can also sidestep areas of particular difficulty. Spare a thought, then, for the translator of Perec's *La Disparition*, Gilbert Adair, whose English version, wittily entitled *A Void* and governed by the exclusion of 'e' as in the original, is necessarily both lengthy and doubly constrained.

If you've enjoyed grappling with lipograms you may want to explore a few exercises that work in similar ways, prompting you, through the imposition of artificial patterns, to think carefully about words and meanings. Consider the following passage, which is restricted to words of one syllable.

> *She thought she would write a tale made of words of just one beat.* 'That will be hard,' *she thought.* 'But it might be fun.'
>
> *Just then her man came through the door with a cup of tea. (Why not a glass of wine? She might have liked that more, but this is how it was.)*
>
> '*What are you up to?*' *he asked.*
> *She told him.*
> '*Write it,*' *he said.*
> '*I think I will,*' *she said.* '*Or, I should say, I'll try.*'

5.
   Now try one or more of the following:

   a) Write your own passage of prose using only words of one syllable, as in the example above.

   b) Write a passage starting with a two-word sentence, following it with a three-word sentence, which is in turn followed by a four-word sentence – and so on until your ingenuity gives out.

   c) Write a paragraph in which every sentence contains the same number of words.

If you enjoyed these exercises in constrained writing you may want to invent and experiment with forms of constraint not represented here; but you've no doubt understood the general principle, and we shall now move on to examine other forms of wordplay.

A bit of the proverbial

There's a category of similes that are, in the broad sense of the term, proverbial; similes of this kind are used to signal that something takes a particularly intense form. We might say that someone was as drunk as a lord, or as cold as ice; or we might promise to be as quiet as a mouse or as good as gold. People shake like leaves, cry like babies or laugh like drains. Similes may be made memorable by alliteration – as busy as a bee, as cool as a cucumber – or by rhyme: as snug as a bug in a rug. Sometimes we invoke a well-known character as the embodiment of a particular quality: as old as Methuselah, as rich as Croesus, as pleased as Punch.

The problem with these familiar similes is that they are also clichés, apt but worn smooth by overuse. As writers we want to avoid cliché, but we also need to avoid straining too hard for novelty, especially in dialogue: it's better to have a character say that his daughter was shaking like a leaf than to have him say that she was shaking like a loose lightbulb in a moving train.

The following exercise invites you to invent new proverbial phrases illustrative of a range of simple qualities.

6.

Complete the phrases below with imaginative illustrations of the qualities listed. You're aiming for a combination of originality, aptness, succinctness and memorability.

As busy as…
As bright as…
As fast as…
As miserable as…
As hot as…
As mad as…
As blunt as…

You may have been surprised by the difficulty of this task – or, at least, the difficulty of doing it well. The problem is that the obvious examples have already been taken, making it hard to tick the box for originality without veering into the realms of the over-ingenious. But if you invented anything that seems to work, file it away: like Raymond Chandler, who kept a list of ready-to-use similes, you never know when it might come in handy.

Proverbial similes of this kind can be differentiated from proverbs, which are pithy sayings embodying a general truth, a nugget of wisdom or a piece of advice; these are usually, in essence, metaphors, transforming more or less abstract ideas into simple concrete images. When you translate proverbs of this kind back into their more abstract meanings you can see why they are so useful: statements such as 'a stitch in time saves nine' or 'a bird in the hand is worth two in the bush' are more economical and more memorable, than 'a small remedial action early on will prevent more extensive measures becoming necessary at a later date', or 'something already in your possession is twice as valuable as something you haven't yet got hold of'. With these examples in mind, you might enjoy the following exercise.

7.

Define, as clearly and as succinctly as you can, the meanings of the following well-known proverbs:

A leopard cannot change its spots
A rolling stone gathers no moss
A watched pot never boils
All that glisters is not gold
The proof of the pudding is in the eating
There's no smoke without fire

And now you might like to try this rather more difficult exercise, which reverses the process.

8.

Invent proverbs that make use of concrete images to embody the following abstract ideas:

The beginning of any enterprise is the hardest part.
Any action can have unintended consequences.
It's easier to acquire bad habits than to lose them.
It's foolish to spend time thinking about the future.
Those who act kindly towards others create happiness for themselves.
It's unwise to talk about matters you don't understand.

Fun with puns

Punning – playing on the double meaning or similar sound of words – is common in everyday conversation: you can probably think of someone in your family or workplace who regularly enlivens conversation with a good pun (or elicits groans with a bad one). And there are many literary examples – as when, in Shakespeare's *Romeo and Juliet*, Romeo rejects Mercutio's suggestion that he should dance at the ball, replying: 'You have dancing shoes/ With nimble soles, I have a soul of lead'; or when Mercutio, mortally wounded, says 'Ask for me tomorrow, and you shall find me a grave man'.

Here's an example of sustained punning in a lighthearted narrative:

> *The joint was a mess. The waitress was slumped on the floor.*
> *'Spill the beans,' I snapped.*
> *'Half a dozen bad eggs started buying rounds of drinks,' she stammered. 'Within an hour the whole place had gone crazy. The onions were pickled. They were picking fights with the other vegetables: the mushrooms got battered.'*
> *A further survey of the room revealed no clues to the whereabouts of the perpetrators, though I noticed that one of the tables was suspiciously reserved. I was getting nowhere fast.*
> *And then I saw something lurking in the doorway, blushing guiltily.*
> *'What is it?' asked the waitress nervously.*
> *I took out my notebook; I had my lead. 'I'm going to grill that tomato,' I replied, licking my pencil.*

This kind of play can be entertaining to read and enjoyable to write. The following exercise invites you to experiment with a version of your own.

9.
Write a passage of prose containing multiple puns. If you want to follow the culinary theme you could write a continuation of the narrative above (the possibilities have by no means been exhausted); or you might prefer to find your own theme.

You probably realised that the passage we gave you has been written in a manner loosely imitative of twentieth-century American detective fiction; we're now going to move on to a form of play more directly focused on the art of imitation.

Imitation games

All writers begin by imitating, to a greater or lesser extent, the works of authors they admire; this is imitation as the sincerest form of flattery. Good writers progress beyond imitation, inevitably indebted to their models but developing their own style and themes; others, continuing in imitative mode, will produce pastiche – work that merely apes the style and themes of others.

Pastiche shades into parody when it's used knowingly and for humorous or satirical effect. Parody depends for its best effects on a detailed knowledge of the writer in question, and it tends to work most effectively when that writer has a highly distinctive style: it's easier to parody Raymond Chandler or D. H. Lawrence than to parody (say) P. D. James or Julian Barnes.

For present purposes we shall be looking at imitations of a looser and less literary kind, requiring no prior knowledge of specific authors. The following paragraphs come from a chapter headed 'Things to Refrain From' in an Edwardian etiquette book:

> Don't wear a number of diamonds or other precious stones by day; it is never in good taste.
>
> Don't use such words as 'elegant', 'chap', 'genteel', 'gents', 'the party that told me', 'a toff', &c., &c.
>
> Don't speak of a person as 'a swell'; keep the expression to apply to the ocean.
>
> Don't cut or bite your bread at lunch or dinner, or make crumbs.
>
> Don't use a spoon to eat a sweet with if you can possibly manage to eat it with a fork. When a fork only is being used it should be held in the right hand.
>
> Don't ask for a second helping of soup or fish.
>
> Don't, if you meet a gentleman smoking a cigar, stop and talk to him, unless you have something of importance to say; as to do so would make it incumbent on him to throw his cigar away, or let it go out, which to him would be almost as bad.
>
> Don't, even at a family meal, lift the forks, spoons, or knives out of the vegetable and other dishes on to your plate. It is quite wrong to do so. It is better to run the risk of the servant dropping them than

to get into so objectionable a habit, but this need never happen if the servant is but ordinarily careful.

Don't wear a fine gown and shabby boots: to do so stamps a woman at once.

This list of prohibitions belongs to another time, another world; it reflects the class and gender relationships prevalent in the age in which it was written and it makes certain assumptions about its readership. In addressing the following exercise you might want to satirise some of these assumptions; more subtly, you might also attempt to mimic the authoritative tone of the advice, and, if you wish, its grammar and punctuation.

10.
Taking the example above as your model, write a passage of guidance for a young twenty-first-century reader. This might also mock the manners of the present age ('Don't hold your iPhone unduly close to your bowl while your father is ladling the soup; this is not merely ill-mannered but may have regrettable results'); or you may use the absurdity – from a modern viewpoint – of some of the etiquette book's advice as inspiration for a list of ridiculous prohibitions ('Don't wear cotton socks with steel-rimmed spectacles; to do so marks a man out as one of life's failures'). And here's a piece of advice from us: Don't worry about getting this task 'right' – just have fun with it.

If you enjoyed that exercise you might like to try working with another form of imitation, essentially a mash-up in which a narrative derived from one source is couched in the terms appropriate to another. In this case we suggest rewriting a familiar folk tale in the style of a newspaper report, taking the following narrative as an example:

LOCAL FAMILY 'DEVASTATED' BY BREAK-IN

Shortly after nine o'clock on Tuesday morning a family of three returned to their home after a short stroll in the forest and discovered an intruder asleep in one of the beds. Items of furniture had been damaged and food stolen.

'We'd left the house unlocked,' said home-owner Robert Bruin, a local leader of the 'Back to Nature' movement and a pillar of his small, close-knit community. 'It has always been a safe neighbourhood – you certainly don't expect this kind of thing.'

His wife, Ursula, was quick to agree. 'Nothing like this has happened here before. But it's a sign of the times, isn't it? And now we have Bobby junior refusing to sleep in his own bed, though goodness knows we've done what we can – cleaned the carpet, changed the sheets, put a bolt on the door. He saw the intruder leave by the window, and he's terrified she'll get back in by the same route. As for getting him to eat out of his porridge bowl…'

Ursula is still tearful when she speaks about the incident. 'It has devastated us,' she says, 'and we won't feel safe until the culprit is behind bars.'

Police renewed their call for witnesses. The suspect – blonde, pink and estimated to be about four feet tall – is still at large.

In this example the emphasis has been shifted from Goldilocks' point of view, as in the traditional version, to that of the bears. In inviting you to approach the narrative from a different perspective, we're also – in light-hearted mode but with serious implications for your writing – encouraging you to think of the variety of viewpoints from which the events of any story may be experienced.

11.

With this example in mind, take another folk tale and treat it as a news report. European tales such as 'Cinderella', 'Hansel and Gretel', 'Jack and the Beanstalk' or 'Little Red Riding Hood', may be obvious choices, but if you're familiar with tales from other traditions you'll perhaps prefer to use those. Adapt details in whatever ways best suit your purpose, thinking about possible shifts of viewpoint: there's creative mileage in representing the viewpoint of an ogre who wakes to find that a young ne'er-do-well has run off with his possessions, or of a wolf whose intended dinner has been snatched from his jaws by her axe-wielding father. Think, too, about the point in time from which the events are reported. Nailing the headline may

be helpful in this respect: a narrative headed 'Prince orders nationwide search for unidentified stunner' will probably look rather different from one headed 'Wedding bells ring out for royal couple'.

In brief

You've probably come across the term 'flash fiction', often used generically to designate all fictions shorter than the typical short story; stories up to 1000 words in length, with a recognisable plot and at least one character, come into that broad category. Within the category a number of sub-categories have been identified or imposed. Since these sub-categories occasionally overlap with each other or are variously defined, and since precise definitions are of doubtful use in the present context, let's keep it simple and use the term 'flash fiction' to include them all.

The term itself is a recent coinage, but very short stories have been around for a long time. The fables attributed to Aesop and first written down in the fourth century BCE are good examples of early short-form fiction; here's one of the best known:

The Hare and the Tortoise

A hare one day ridiculed the short legs and slow pace of a tortoise, who said with a laugh: 'Though you be swift as the wind, I will beat you in a race.' The hare, believing this to be impossible, assented to the proposal and they agreed that the fox should choose the course and fix the goal.

On the day appointed for the race the two started together. The tortoise set off immediately and went on with a slow but steady pace to the end of the course. The hare, trusting to his natural speed, lay down for a nap by the wayside. When he woke, he set off and ran as fast as he could, but discovered the tortoise had reached the goal, and was comfortably dozing after her tiring efforts.

Simple, succinct and memorable, these fables also have a moral, which in many printed versions appears in the form of a proverb at the conclusion of each tale. It's an addition that we might normally regard as unnecessary: the fable has already shown us what the appended moral, hammering home a point we should be able to work out for ourselves, merely tells us. However, the next exercise invites you to consider the moral as the starting point for an illustrative tale.

12.

Taking 'The Hare and the Tortoise' as your model, write your own fable in 150 words or fewer. Choose your moral from those below, or use any other proverb as the basis for your story.

A chain is only as strong as its weakest link
A little learning is a dangerous thing
Charity begins at home
Good things come to those who wait

The Aesopian model was probably helpful to you in certain respects as you addressed this exercise, but you may wish now to work with greater freedom; the next exercise invites you to do so.

13.

Write a story of your own, of any length between 100 and 1000 words. Many plots and themes are too complex to be readily contained in a piece of flash fiction, so it will be worth giving a little thought to your subject before you start writing.

Like other forms of constraint discussed earlier in this section, the strictly limited wordcount may have prevented you from exercising your skills to the full; and whatever your own experience with this particular task it's fair to say that, notwithstanding some notable exceptions (for example, the sharply observed work of Lydia Davis or the tightly written pieces in Simon Armitage's collection *Seeing Stars*), flash fiction can often seem shallow and underdeveloped. However, the form provides one of the most useful resources for developing writers wishing to practise their craft on a small scale, in the way apprentice cabinet makers used to hone their skills on miniature versions of the furniture they would later be making full size.

The following three exercises invite you to work under similar constraints with regard to wordcount, but with complications that will further exercise your ingenuity.

14.
Your task is to write the text of three postcards, each to a maximum of 100 words. There are two correspondents, A and B (you can decide on their names and the nature of their relationship). Correspondent A, on holiday, sends correspondent B a card; B sends a card in response; A replies. These three cards should allow you to tell a very short story, in the voices of your two characters; try to let that story emerge obliquely from the correspondence rather than being too obviously its subject.

Now, under similar wordcount constraints, try working with this complication.

15.
This time all three postcards come from the same person. The other side of the correspondence has been lost. Your task is to construct a narrative that gives us subtle clues not only about the writer but also about the addressee and the content of the lost side of the correspondence.

The final exercise is more ambitious, and you may want to address it in sections, adding an item or two each day. It invites you to work cumulatively, through a sequence of brief, interrelated narratives, to provide a miniature portrait of a village and its inhabitants.

16.
Depict a village community by creating a few pages of a fictional parish magazine or community newsletter, using various headings as listed below. The aim is to suggest, using no more than 100 words for each headed item, a story or situation which no single item provides in full, but which the reader is able to put together from the sum of the evidence supplied. Make use of any or all of the following categories, typical of such publications:

Editorial
Message from a representative of the local church or other religious institution
Reports from various village organisations
Special interest columns (for example, gardening, cookery, D.I.Y)
Notices of events and activities
Births, marriages and deaths
Advertisements for local businesses

As you've worked your way through this section you'll have been aware of the various writerly skills necessarily involved in addressing the tasks you've been set, and you'll have understood experientially that even the most playful of exercises may provide insights important to your development as a serious writer. Equally, you may have discovered or rediscovered, through these forms of wordplay, a heightened ease or fluency in your writing, and a deeper understanding of the value of experimentation.

In this book's predecessor, *The Book You Need to Read to Write the Book You Want to Write*, we suggested that a willingness to experiment is essential to the writer's development, and that there may be as much to be learned from the experiments that fail as from those that succeed. In the present book we've encouraged you to view your responses to the prompts in the same light – as steps on a journey rather than as ends in themselves. That journey is a continuing process, and this book, like its predecessor, is designed to serve you as a writer far beyond your first reading. We hope it will be your companion for as long as you find it useful, and that you might return to it whenever you feel in need of guided practice, helpful advice or simply an incentive to get on with the business of writing.

For EU product safety concerns, contact us at Calle de José Abascal, 56–1°,
28003 Madrid, Spain or eugpsr@cambridge.org.

www.ingramcontent.com/pod-product-compliance
Lightning Source LLC
LaVergne TN
LVHW011826060526
838200LV00053B/3910